Designing and Developing Electronic Performance Support Systems

Designing and Developing Electronic Performance Support Systems

Lesley A. Brown

Digital Press
Boston Oxford Melbourne Singapore Toronto Munich New Delhi Tokyo

Digital Press™ is an imprint of Butterworth-Heinemann
℞ A member of the Reed Elsevier group

 Recognizing the importance of preserving what has been written, Butterworth-
Heinemann prints its books on acid-free paper whenever possible.

Trademarked products mentioned in this book are listed on the back page.

Library of Congress Cataloging-in-Publication Data

Brown, Lesley (Lesley A.). 1961-
    Designing and developing electronic performance support systems /
by Lesley Brown.
        p.   cm.
    Includes index
    ISBN 1-55558-139-0 (alk. paper)
        1. Employees--Training of--Computer-assisted instruction.
    2. Computer software--Development. 3. Computer-assisted
    instruction--Design. I. Title.
    HF5549.5.T7B733 1995
    658.3′12404--dc20

The publisher offers discounts on bulk orders of this book.
For information, please write:

Manager of Special Sales, Digital Press
Butterworth–Heinemann
313 Washington Street
Newton, MA 02158–1626

Order number: EY–T126E–DP

10 9 8 7 6 5 4 3 2 1

Printed in the United States of America

Contents

Preface

The History of This Book

Electronic Performance Support Systems (EPSS) is a concept that integrates work tasks with on-line support. Like most companies on the cutting edge of technology, Digital Equipment Corporation has several teams of visionaries who are creating these state-of-the art systems.

In 1993, the management team of the Information Design and Consulting (IDC) group and the Digital Learning Services organization decided to document the process that a team of training professionals used to create an EPSS called the Learning Services Workbench. The team used an instructional systems design approach called D^4M^2: Define, Design, Develop, and Deliver; Manage-Measure (redefined and expanded in this book to a process called ED^4: EPSS Define, Design, Develop, and Deliver).

The D^4M^2 Process

The D^4M^2 process is an instructional systems design process which was developed in the 1980s by Digital's Educational Services organization. This process provides the steps, checkpoints, tips, and tools to create an instructional product. Instructional designers and course developers within Educational Services used this process to create products ranging from lecture/labs, and self-paced print instruction to computer-based training.

The process, which is based on instructional systems theory and methodology, includes four phases – Define, Design, Develop, and Deliver. Overriding the tasks included in these phases are project management tasks (Manage-Measure).

Key components of the D^4M^2 process are:

- Project planning and scheduling

- Quality checkpoints of instructional materials within the team and with the client and target audience

- Documentation of the project (project plans, design specifications, and so on)

- Ongoing assessment of the instructional materials' validity with the target audience through prototyping, pilot testing, and so on.

EPSS at Digital Equipment Corporation

This book focuses on the process used by the Learning Services Workbench development team, with contributions from the Sales Horizon and Sales PowerPack! design and development teams.

The Learning Services Workbench

The Learning Services Workbench was created in 1993 by a cross-functional team of instructional designers, graphic designers, software engineers, course developer/writers, video producers, quality assurance experts, and subject matter experts. The team used the D^4M^2 process.

The profile of the Learning Services Workbench is:

- **Goal**
  Provide on-line tools, information, and resources that are integrated into a core business process and delivered on a laptop personal computer.

- **Audience**
  Learning Services consultants who provide customized training to customers outside of Digital Equipment Corporation.

- **User Needs and Workbench Responses**
  - Modular proposal database
  - Access to PC-based tools and applications
  - Reference information
  - Customer presentation material
  - Software demos

Sales Horizons

Sales Horizon was created to provide a mobile performance support tool for sales people who uses laptop PCs to sell to customers. A key component of Sales Horizon is the ability to connect to Digital's network, request information or support, disconnect, and reconnect at a later date to retrieve the information or support.

The design and development team used an iterative development approach. The team created the base system, then added functionality via frequent interaction with users.

Sales PowerPack!

A Sales PowerPack! provides access to sales information, proposals, and demonstrations. Employing hypertext technology, PowerPacks provide just-in-time information for sales people.

Book Layout

Structure

This book consists of three parts and eleven chapters as described below.

Part		Chapter	Description
1	Understand the EPSS Concept	What is Electronic Performance Support?	Defines and describes the EPSS concept
		Choosing EPSS as the Performance Solution	Differentiates between EPSS and training
		Justifying EPSS	Provides justification

Part		Chapter	Description
			for EPSS investment
2	Prepare for EPSS Design and Development	Building an EPSS Development Team	Identifies EPSS design team members
		Looking at EPSS Technology	Overviews EPSS hardware and software
3	A Process for EPSS Design and Development	ED^4: A Design and Development Approach	Overviews the ED^4 process phases
		ED^4: The Define Phase	
		ED^4: The Design Phase	
		ED^4: The Develop Phase	
		ED^4: The Deliver Phase	
		Maintaining EPSS	Describes support and maintenance strategies

Conventions

This book uses the following conventions.

Tool Icon

Within the book, the tool icon below identifies checklists, guidelines, descriptions and so on for EPSS design, development, and maintenance.

Project Management Checkpoints

Chapters 7–10 describe the phases of the ED^4 process. At the end of each of these chapters is a section called "Project Manage the Phase." This section describes key project management checkpoints where the project manager should:

- **Manage**
  These are either people or process patterns that the project manager should establish or maintain. For example, in *Chapter 7:*

The Define Phase, the project manager sets client expectations by involving the client in reviews of project specifications.

- **Document**
  These are important documents about the EPSS design, team process, and client contract that the project manager creates and adds to an on- or off-line project file.

Overcoming Obstacles Summaries

Chapters 7–10 describe the phases of the ED^4 process. At the end of each of these chapters is a section called "Overcoming Obstacles." This section describes common problems during the phase as articulated by EPSS designers and developers, and solutions for these problems.

Terminology

The following terminology is used in this book.

Performers

The group or groups of people for whom the EPSS is created. Conventional training and software engineering refers to this group as the "end users," "users," or "target audience." Performance technologists use the word "performer" to concentrate on the person and task, rather than the software.

EPSS Team

Used in this book to represent the EPSS design and EPSS development team or teams.

EPSS Elements

A category of EPSS response to a performer request for job task support.

Acknowledgments

The following people were critical to the direction, content, design, and scope of this book:

- The Learning Services Workbench EPSS development team who used the ED^4 process to create the Workbench and on whose work this book is based: Marion Hamblett, Rachel Pantely, Marie Piantedosi, Phyllis Simpson, Karen Nisbet, Byron Braxton, Rachel Oulette, Andrea Ting, Jack Jurras, Liz Ronai, Jonathan George, and Corrine Hamilton.

- The dedicated group of EPSS architects, designers, developers, and managers at Digital Equipment Corporation who reviewed this book for technical accuracy and educational quality. In the United States: Marion Hamblett, Bill Dibbern, Jim Nuzzo, Roger Bowker, Joyce Thomas, Ken Wadowski, Mitch Grossberg, Arthur Shirk, and Dale Hines. In Europe: Charles Revkin, Peter Leonard, and Sally-Ann Moore.

- The EPSS developers at Consultec in Boston for reviewing the manuscript and talking with me about their experiences: Jennifer Lippincott, David Warboth, and Ben Spector.

- Special thanks to Gloria Gery for devoting her precious spare time for review and comments on Chapter One. Unfortunately, the deadline prohibited me from incorporating all of her comments. Ms. Gery is on the leading edge of EPSS, and her contributions to the field of electronic performance support are immeasurable.

- Visionaries from the now defunct Educational Services Development & Publishing (ESD&P) group at Digital Equipment Corporation who created the D^4M^2 design and development process which the ED^4 process is based on.

- Marion Hamblett, the key visionary for the Learning Services Workbench for her dedication to this book.

- Karen Andersen, Karn Ryken, and Janice Cassin for fighting to get the funding to complete the writing of this book.

- Arthur Shirk for the wonderful idea of capturing the work of the Learning Services Workbench team.

- Shan Mahendren and Jim Stewart of Digital's Learning Services organization for providing the support and funding to write this book.

- Mike Dempsey of DePubs Consulting, Whitinsville, MA, for the beautiful book design, layout, and first set of graphics, and Ray Laurencelle of Digital Equipment Corporation's Media Design group for the final set of graphics.

And last but not least, I thank my husband Jeffrey for his support, encouragement and research assistance and my children, Rayna, Lauren, and Aaron for letting their Mommy create this book.

Understand the EPSS Concept

1

PART

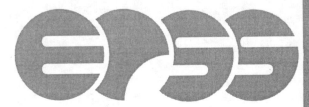

What Is Electronic Performance Support?

THIS CHAPTER describes the concept of Electronic Performance Support System (EPSS), defines and describes the elements that make up EPSS, and provides some examples of EPSS.

Example of a performance problem and the EPSS solution.

A Typical Day with EPSS

An EPSS can increase the efficiency and productivity of a bank manager by providing all of the tools the manager needs to perform job tasks (see Figure 1-1).

A Bank Manager's Dilemma

You are a bank branch manager preparing to write a performance appraisal for an employee. You're nervous because you're new to your job and this is your first performance appraisal. To complicate matters further, this employee is due for a promotion, and you've never completed promotion paperwork before.

Where should you begin? Should you call your supervisor and ask for help? Shouldn't there be a personnel manual to help you figure this out? Isn't there a course on writing appraisals?

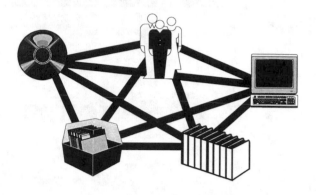

Figure 1-1. EPSS Elements

Solving the Dilemma with EPSS

Then you remember that your supervisor mentioned there is an on-line support system called Performance Appraisal System (PAS). You log on to PAS (see Figure 1-2). The system requests your name, job title, and the name of the person you are reviewing. You supply the information.

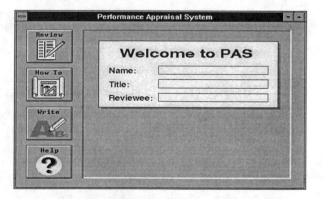

Figure 1-2. Performance Appraisal System Welcome Screen

Acts as an Advisor

Automatically, a window pops up reminding you that this employee received an award this year for outstanding work performance. The pop-up message *advises* you to review this information (Figure 1-3). You decide this is a good idea and read the information in another window on the screen.

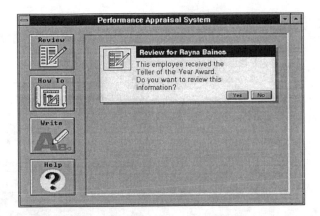

Figure 1-3. PAS Advisor Screen

Provides a Learning Experience and Help

After reading the award information, you prepare to write the review. You note that there is a short *learning module* on how to write performance appraisals (see Figure 1-4). You take the module, branching out via the *help button* to read definitions of terms and see examples of other appraisals.

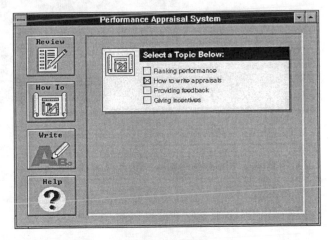

Figure 1-4. Access to Learning Module

Provides Customized Application Software

Now you're ready to write. You click on the Write Appraisal icon. The system asks you a series of questions about the employee, which you answer. The system opens up *word processing software* containing the performance appraisal form (see Figure 1-5). You see the information you supplied about the employee entered into the form. Certain phrases in the template are highlighted. Clicking on these phrases gives you advice on what you should write.

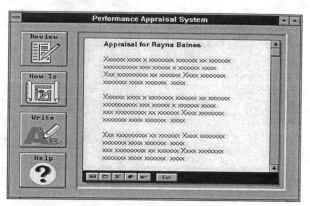

Figure 1-5. Performance Appraisal

Monitors Actions

You complete the appraisal form and start to log out of PAS. A message warns you that you have not saved the appraisal form. The message asks you if the form should be saved and printed (see Figure 1-6). You respond "yes," and the system performs these tasks.

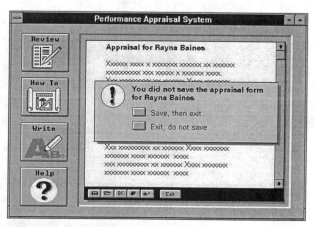

Figure 1-6. Warning Message

Assesses Actions

PAS *assesses* the work you've done so far and recommends that you view a short video on delivering performance appraisals. You click on the Start Video button and watch different managers deliver performance appraisals (see Figure 1-7).

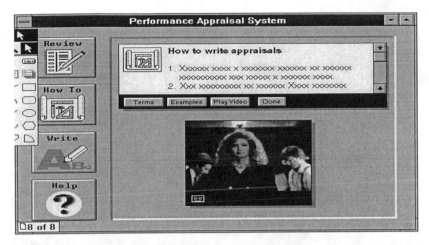

Figure 1-7. Video on Performance Appraisals

PAS Is an EPSS

The Performance Appraisal System (PAS) used by the bank manager is an Electronic Performance Support System. Everything the bank manager needed to create a performance appraisal was available and integrated. The manager did not have to call a supervisor or coworker, consult a manual on a bookshelf, or go to an off-site training course. No valuable work time was lost searching for information or waiting for assistance.

Definition of EPSS

An **Electronic Performance Support System (EPSS)** is a software environment that provides, "a context within which work is done. Everything needed to do the job – information, software, expert advice and guidance, and learning experiences – is integrated and available, resulting in improved worker productivity and minimal support and intervention by others."[1] (See Figure 1-8.)

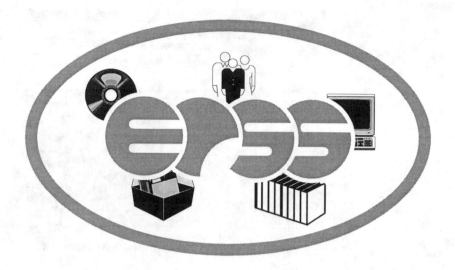

Figure 1-8. EPSS Elements

What EPSS Is

EPSS is a concept. It is a shift away from viewing workers as "people to be trained" to viewing workers as "people who need support on the job." It is a new way of viewing the work environment. An EPSS concentrates on the employee (hereafter referred to as the *performer*), the job and the job tasks.

As performers learn new or complex tasks, they ask questions or request help. The EPSS software attempts to anticipate questions and requests and provides the appropriate advice and help.

Gery looked at the questions performers ask and the requests they make when they are tackling a job task. Table 1-1 gives the questions that performers ask and requests they make and possible responses of an EPSS. [2]

Table 1-1. Performer Needs/Requests and EPSS Responses

The Question or Need	Response of Performance Support System
Why do this?	Explanation
	Example and consequences
What is it?	Definitions
	Illustrations
	Descriptions
What's related to it?	Available links

The Question or Need	Response of Performance Support System
How do I do it?	Procedure
	Interactive advisors
	Structured paths (flowcharts, step charts, job aids)
	Demonstration
How or why did this happen?	Explanation
	Example or demonstration
Show me an example...	Examples
Teach me...	Interactive training
	Practice activities with feedback
	Assessment or testing
Assist me...	Interactive advisors
Advise me...	Structured paths, job aids, step charts, flowcharts
	Monitoring systems with feedback
Let me try...	Practice activities
	Simulations
Watch me...	Practice activities
	Simulations
Evaluate me...	Assessments or tests
Understand me...	Feedback with scoring, judgment, or interpretation
	Monitoring systems tracking user actions or context
How does it work?	Explanations
Why does it work like that?	Examples
Compare this or these for me...	Comparative explanations or descriptions
Predict for me...	Descriptions or demonstrations of consequences
Where am I?	Monitoring systems
	Navigation systems
	Views of context ("you are here...")
What next?	Directions, prompts, or coaching
	Lists of options or paths

EPSS Goals

Performers have specific needs when performing job tasks. A well-designed EPSS meets these needs. While not an exhaustive list, some of the more important goals of a well-designed EPSS are:

- **Provide electronic support for the job tasks**
  The EPSS should provide help, demonstrations, advice, customized templates, access to databases, or any other support that the performer needs to perform a task or series of tasks.

  For example, an EPSS for a copy editor could include customized software for inserting electronic proofreading symbols into a review copy. An on-line version of the relevant style guide (such as the *Chicago Manual of Style*) with hypertext explanations could provide the editor with the appropriate editing standard.

- **Integrate the support into the work environment**
  The task and the EPSS should be tightly linked, that is, the support should be an integral part of the task. Performers should be able to access or be given support as they perform tasks.

  For example, a tax analyst who is doing an on-line tax return could access an on-line version of the tax code rather than the multi-volume printed reference. A more tightly integrated EPSS would provide the relevant tax code sections or warn the analysts about conflicts between the code and the tax return as the analyst enters information into the tax return form. Tax return information such as the customer's name, address, profession, and marital status would automatically be filled in on any tax form for this customer.

- **Provide support on demand**
  The support should be "just-in-time." The EPSS gives exactly what the performers need when they need it. The performer should not have to: wait for a response; get the wrong or no response; or refer to people or other off-line resources.

  Support should be in the format that the performer needs. For example, an EPSS for a word processing system could include help on creating a table of contents. An elaborate EPSS might include several forms of assistance like hypertext links to reference information, a short CBT module on creating table of contents, and a choice of customized table of content formats.

- **Use technology as needed**
  EPSSs exist that use technology extensively, and EPSSs exist that do not. If the task, performer or work environment requires it, the EPSS should supply it. Technology that EPSSs use include

software technologies such as hypermedia, multimedia, graphic user interfaces (GUIs), computer-based training, expert systems and hardware technologies such as CD-ROM, audio, and networks.

Appropriate use of technology is critical. For example, suppose an EPSS were needed to support bank tellers who have minimal computer knowledge and limited access to very rudimentary PC software. The EPSS could be implemented in phases – the first phase of the software could support a basic task like verifying a customer's identity using a simple question-based, hypertext job aid. Subsequent phases could use more sophisticated technology like an expert system to guide the tellers through the process.

How the EPSS Concept Evolved

The EPSS concept evolved from companies' changing needs for improving job performance and from the proliferation of technology.

Companies' Changing Needs

Today's businesses face many challenges. A primary challenge is keeping the skills of their employees up-to-date. Classroom training has been an important mode of maintaining and increasing employee skills. However, many companies are looking for alternative methods for influencing the performance of their workers. Training budgets are being cut. Businesses can no longer afford to send their employees away for training.

Many businesses are looking for on-the-job options to aid skill transfer. EPSSs address this need. EPSSs exist on the desktop and employees can get the kind of help they need for job tasks when they need it.

Chapter 2, *Choosing EPSS as the Performance Solution*, describes additional reasons for the interest and need for EPSS.

Changing Technology

The technology exists to make EPSS a reality. Personal computers sit on many employees' desks. Sophisticated mainframes provide networking capability for these PCs. These systems open the door to multimedia, hypermedia, graphics, graphic user interfaces and many other technologies that are EPSS building blocks.

These technologies have been available for many years as stand-alone options. However, recent developments in software and hardware have changed this. These technologies may now be integrated.[3] Microsoft software applications are a good example. Microsoft Word documents can include Excel spreadsheets, call up hyptertext help from knowledge base, and be cut and pasted into all of the Microsoft Office products.

EPSSs capitalize on the integration of all of these exciting technologies.

Need for On-Line Support

EPSSs are improving work performance in a multitude of prof-essions. Sales representatives, manufacturing workers, software developers, and field engineers are using EPSS successfully. EPSSs can support a single performer group or many integrated performer groups.

EPSSs exist on a wide range of hardware/software platforms. The complexity of EPSS implementations range from simple standalone information databases to complex, integrated systems. The tasks that EPSSs support can be simple or complex. See Table 1-6 for examples of performer groups that are benefiting from the EPSS concept.

Instructional and Systems Design

EPSS design should link instructional and systems design.

Besides the industry demands for performance-based, desktop job support, the linking of two professions has made EPSS design and development a reality. EPSS is a concept that incorporates the best of two key professional disciplines (see Figure 1-9):

- **Instructional design**
  Involves defining, designing, developing and delivering generic, job-specific, and product-specific instructional and inform-ational material. Instructional designers develop course and informational materials using print (hardcopy), audio-visual, computer-based instruction, multimedia, and interactive video techniques.

- **Systems design**
  Involves planning, writing, testing, and correcting the steps required for a computer to solve a problem or perform an operation. Systems designers and developers create software systems.

Figure 1-9. EPSS Design Includes Instructional Design (ID) and Systems Design (SD)

Experts in these fields realize that good EPSS design means creating a methodology that embraces both disciplines. "While there are overlaps among and between the methodologies, [instructional design and system design as] a new methodology and discipline will have to be forged from the best and most appropriate components of each."[4] In EPSS design methodology, instructional design (ID) emphasizes job and task performance. Instructional designers and systems designers work together to create an environment that permits optimal job performance.

Table 1-2 describes the expertise that instructional designers and systems designers bring to EPSS design and development.

Table 1-2. ID and SD Expertise

Instructional Design	System Design
Job, task, and needs analyses	Requirements analysis
User interface design	User interface design
Learning strategy design	Technological requirements
EPSS component identification	System analysis and design
Performer (user) testing	System creation
Information design	System integration and testing

Aspects of an EPSS

In EPSS, *whether* the system responds to a performer need is as important as *how* the system responds. For example, a performer who is creating a performance appraisal may not realize that an expert system and modular learning experience are working "behind the scenes." The performer only knows that the information or support for the task is *available*. However, it is easier to understand the EPSS concept by looking at the type of responses the EPSS can provide.

An EPSS includes one, several, or all of the following aspects (hereafter referred to as *components*):

- Task logic
- Knowledge bases
- Support resources
- Data
- Tools
- User interface

Task Logic

Gery emphasizes that an EPSS must include task logic. Task logic is "the sequences, relationships, interrelationships, calculations, etc. associated with successful task completion."[5]

Performers often use incorrect or incomplete logic when they perform a task.[6] For example, a writer who is using Microsoft Word might mistakenly use a Microsoft Word table to create a bar graph instead of using the proper tool, Microsoft Excel. The EPSS prevents mistakes like this by building task logic into the software and providing support and feedback for tasks. For example, if the writer started creating a graph using MS Word, the EPSS could display a pop-up window to recommend Microsoft Excel as the best solution for creating graphs.

Examples of Task Logic

Microsoft Wizards and Cue Cards are examples of incorporating task logic into software.

- **Wizards**
  These are self-contained, automation of commonly performed tasks. Wizards provide performers with options for performing a task. The wizard asks questions which shape the final pro-duct. For example, Microsoft Word offers a Resume Wizard as shown in Figure 1-10. Using a series of questions, and providing layout options, the wizard creates a customized resume.

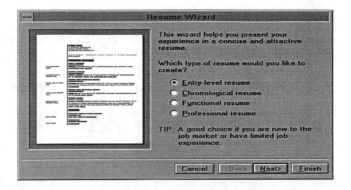

Figure 1-10. Microsoft Word: Resume Wizard

- **Cue Cards**

  Cue Cards are like flash cards that appear as performers are using the software. They can contain instructions, procedures, advice, examples, graphics, or links to help topics as shown in Figure 1-11. Cue Card creator Cyndi Bieniek describes the concept, "What we're trying to do is lead you down a path. Cue Cards tell what's available, what you can do, and why you'd want to do it. Then they give you a choice. When you've made the choice, the Cue Card takes you to the right information."[7]

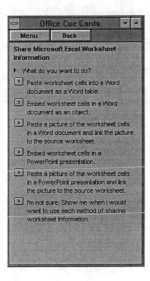

Figure 1-11. Microsoft Cue Card

Building Task Logic into the EPSS

Gery describes different ways that EPSS developers can build task logic into the software as shown in Table 1-3.

Table 1-3. Incorporating Task Logic in EPSS

Task Logic Within the EPSS Is...	Logic Is...	An Example of This Is...
In highly structured forms	System controlled	
Minimally represented	User controlled	Microsoft Wizards, Cue Cards
Invisible (behind the scenes)	System controlled	
Visible	Linear	Microsoft Wizards
	Conditional	Microsoft Cue Cards

Knowledge Bases

Knowledge bases are the representation and storage or non-quantitative data or information.[8]

Knowledge Types

Knowledge represented in an EPSS includes the types in Table 1-4[9].

Table 1-4. Representing Knowledge in an EPSS

Knowledge		Example of EPSS Representation
Concepts	Precipitation	Pop-up window or hypertext link to concept
Facts	Water is wet	Pop-up window containing the fact
Principles	Water at high elevations should fall from the sky	Pop-up window of principle with application to job task
Structures	Diagram of water (H_2O)	Graphic diagram with hypertext links to additional information
Procedures	Steps to purify water	Interactive procedure in text, video, or graphic format

Knowledge		Example of EPSS Representation
Classification	Comparing rain and purified water	Pop-up window of comparison or advisor for recommended path
Processes	What happens during water purification	Interactive or static representation of process in text, video, or graphic format

Knowledge Representation

Knowledge can be stored in a database outside of the EPSS and within different support resources.

Support Resources

Support resources are types of support that the EPSS provides. Note that there may be multiple formats. For example, the process of creating a performance appraisal can be represented in a textual procedure, a video, and a graphic procedure map with hypertext links to a knowledge base.

Formats

Support may be in one or multiple formats:

- **Text**
  Knowledge can be in straight textual form.

- **Hypertext**
  Hypertext is the linking of text in one place in a computer document or knowledge base with another place in the same or different document or knowledge base. The link may provide additional or related information about the original text. Hypertext provides quick, non-linear access to information.

  Performers can browse concepts, facts, principles, and so on from the knowledge base. According to Whiteside and Whiteside, a well-designed knowledge base, "enables users to quickly navigate the structure, find relevant information presented in ways to facilitate comprehension, and return to the departure point with a minimum of confusion."[10]

- **Hypermedia**
  Hypermedia is nonlinear, linked, performer-controlled access to knowledge that is in multimedia format. Multimedia format includes graphics (still or animated), video, and audio.

- **Multimedia**
  Multimedia includes graphics (still or animated), video, and audio. Multimedia in a knowledge base may stand alone. For example, a sales clerk may access and view a complete video on using the cash register from a pull-down menu. Multimedia may also be tightly linked to a job task (hypermedia). For example, the sales clerk may click a button and view the section of the cash register video on handling a credit card sales return while processing the merchandise return.

Types

Support resources may be in one or multiple types:

- **Reference**
  Performers access reference information as they need it. The knowledge the performer receives may or may not be within the context of a task. For example, a software engineer who is curious about object-oriented design (OOD) could access the knowledge base and read a description on OOD.

- **Help**
  Performers access help from the within the context of the task. For example, a writer who is creating a cross-reference to a table would access the knowledge base for a procedure on creating cross-references. The writer would simultaneously read and perform the procedure.

- **Instruction**
  Performers request different types of instruction from the database. Examples of instruction are demos of a procedure, static or hypertext displays of concepts or facts, and stand-alone modules.

- **Coaches**
  Coaches guide performers through a procedure, a decision or series of decisions, or a task. Microsoft Wizards and Cue Cards are examples of coaches. For example, the Resume Wizard in Microsoft Word ask performers a series of questions to help shape the look and contents of a customized resume.

  Expert systems may or may not be the technology that is typically behind coaches.

Data

Data refer to any representation of facts or instructions in a form suitable for communication, interpretation or processing.[11]

Information that the performer supplies or responses the performer gives become data within the EPSS. The system shares these data with other subsystems within the EPSS. If a sales representative includes a customer contact name and address in a contract, that contact information becomes part of a database. Other parts of the EPSS have access to these data. For example, if the sales representative sends a letter to the customer, the EPSS extracts the contact name and address from the database and inserts it in the letter.

The EPSS may extract data from the databases of other software applications. The EPSS then uses these data. For example, EPSSs at Digital Equipment Corporation extract data such as sales information from the corporate database server. The EPSSs use and act on these data.

The EPSS may also pass data created in the EPSS on to external systems. For example, data created in Microsoft Word are available via the database to all other Microsoft Office applications.

Tools

Tools within an EPSS include utilities, applications software, productivity tools, and templates.[12] Tools can be applications software that are used as is, or custom-built software that is integrated into the EPSS. Table 1-5 defines tools as described by Gery.

Table 1-5. Types of Tools in EPSS

Performer...	EPSS Uses Tool as a/an...	Example
Sees and uses tool	Distinct environment	Performer or EPSS opens calculators, spreadsheets, and graphic tools within the EPSS
Operates within the options presented by the tool	Interface, but not distinct environment	Writer enters data into a Microsoft FAX Wizard. The Wizard is a tool that is submerged in the EPSS
Does not see tool	Defined environment for data manipulation, but not a distinct environment	Sales representative sees a sales contract on the screen, but a spreadsheet tool and word processing software are behind the scenes

User Interface

Consider a homeowner that buys a build-it-yourself home entertainment unit. The unit includes separate compartments for the

VCR and stereo components, a rotating base for the television, and recessed storage for compact discs. The homeowner excitedly unpacks the unit, but in dismay, realizes that the instructions and diagrams for how to use the unit are completely incomprehensible. The homeowner discards the instructions and builds the unit anyway. The completed unit has problems, and the homeowner cannot figure out how to use many of its features.

User interfaces provide the access to the EPSS components. They are the screen or series of screens that the performers interact with to inquire, navigate, or receive support from the EPSS. User interfaces are as critical to using an EPSS as excellent instructions are to assembling a home entertainment unit. If the performers cannot understand how to navigate the EPSS to get the support they need, they may discard the software altogether.

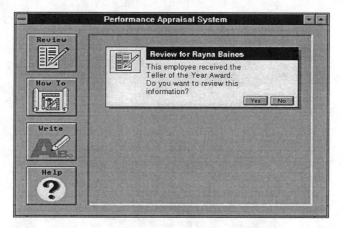

Figure 1-12. User Interface: PAS

Figure 1-12 shows the user interface for a fictitious EPSS called the Performance Appraisal System, a system to assist bank managers in creating performance appraisals. Notice that the buttons on the left are large, easy to read and understand, and that the types of support the EPSS provides is obvious. This is an example of a graphic user interface – it employs graphics and window-based PC elements to receive input and provide output. User interfaces can also be created for non-PC-based systems.

EPSS Examples

Electronic Performance Support Systems vary from one performer situation to another since they match a performer group's unique needs. Different performer needs can support different EPSS implementations. Table 1-6 shows examples of EPSS at Digital Equipment Corporation.

Table 1-6. EPSS Examples at Digital Equipment Corporation

Name of EPSS	Performer Needs	EPSS Elements
Learning Services Workbench	Learning Services consultants need: • Access to proposal writing tools and templates • Understanding of the consulting process • Reminders to save and print important documents • Software demos • Mobile computing	Learning Services Workbench provides: Application and productivity software: Customized, interactive proposal writing templates with guidance statements and direct access to reference or "boilerplate" text Information databases: Hypertext information Monitoring and assessment systems Modular learning experiences: multimedia software demos
Sales Horizons	Sales representatives need: • Mobile computing • Access to sales information from Digital network • Access to information on products	Sales Horizons provides: Ability to request information from the network, disconnect, reconnect, and retrieve information Information databases: full access to Digital's networked information Modular learning experiences: 10 minute, computer-based training modules on products

Name of EPSS	Performer Needs	EPSS Elements
Sales Power Pack!	Sales representatives need: • Easy access to information • Access to product information	Sales PowerPack! provides: Information databases: easy-to-use hypertext information Modular learning experiences: computer-based training integrated into hypertext information and multimedia slide shows

The Range of Support Systems

Electronic performance support systems come in all shapes and sizes. A system can range from a help file that the performer accesses to answer a question, to a fully integrated support environment that includes a graphical user interface, application software, learning experiences, and an expert system to guide the performer.

EPSS can be simple or complex, generalized or customized, legacy or new systems.

Defining characteristics of an EPSS relate directly to the support for the performer. The EPSS should integrate with tasks, (tightly or loosely) and provide the support on an as-needed basis. If integration, quality, completeness, and relevance to the functions of the performer's job are present, the system is functioning as an EPSS.

Comparisons that show the range of EPSS implementation include:

- Simple to complex
- Generalized or customized
- Legacy or new

Simple to Complex

The types and formats of the support that an EPSS provides, and to some degree the software and hardware implementation, determine its complexity.

Support Types Available

The number of formats available to performers will vary with the complexity of the EPSS. For example, a simple EPSS may only include text and simple graphics. A more complex EPSS may include full-motion video.

Support Formats Available

More complex EPSSs provide multiple contexts for the same task. For example, a complex EPSS for auto salespeople might provide video instruction on selling techniques, a "coach" to guide the salesperson through the sale, and a hypertext job aid on countering objections during the sales pitch.

Hardware and Software

Simple and complex systems exist on traditional mainframes as well as personal computer, client/server environments. Complex EPSSs more closely integrate the support and the task which typically involve more complex hardware and more intricate software programming. In addition, integrating different support contexts, (coaches, help, instruction, and so on) can involve multiple programming languages and authoring systems.

Figure 1-13 and 1-14 illustrate simple and complex EPSSs. *Aspects of an EPSS,* covered the topic.

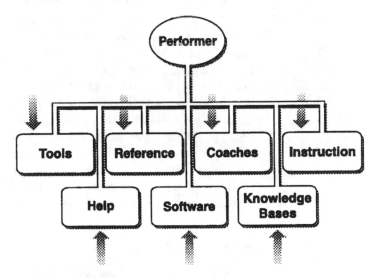

Figure 1-13. A Simple EPSS

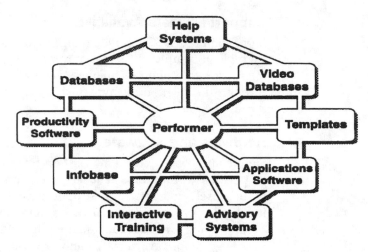

Figure 1-14. A Complex EPSS

Generalized or Customized

A *generalized EPSS* may include off-the-shelf software linked together through a user interface and information-sharing capabilities. For example, an EPSS for a writer may provide easy physical access (through a user interface) to off-the-shelf word processing software, graphic design tools and editing tools.

A *customized EPSS* may tailor off-the-shelf application software to specific job tasks or add links to related software. For example, an EPSS for salespeople could link an off-the-shelf address book software to a customer information database. Customized EPSSs could also include software that is created especially for the performer group. For example, an EPSS for salespeople could add software to pull customer information from a database.

Legacy or New

Corporations can apply the EPSS concept to an existing or legacy system, or they can create new support environments. Legacy systems tend to have outdated hardware and software, cumbersome user interfaces, or use dated programming techniques. Applying the EPSS concept may mean adding a more intuitive user interface, providing better information on how to perform tasks using the system, or organizing system options in the way the performers use them. EPSS designers often apply the concept to a legacy system to convince customers of the concept's merits.

While updating a legacy system is a valid approach in some customer situations, the remainder of this book describes the approach for creating new support environments.

1 Gery, Gloria J., Designing Electronic Performance Support Systems Workshop, Cambridge, Mass., Ziff Institute, 1993.

2 Gery, Gloria J. *Electronic Performance Support Systems: How and Why to Remake the Workplace Through the Strategic Application of Technology*, Boston: Weingarten, 1991.

3 Gery, Gloria J., Electronic Performance Support Systems: How and Why to Remake the Workplace Through the Strategic Application of Technology, Boston: Weingarten, 1991.

4 Gery, Gloria J., "Training vs. Performance Support: Inadequate Training Is Now Insufficient," *Performance Improvement Quarterly*, vol. 2, no. 3, 1989.

5 Gery, Gloria J., Designing Electronic Performance Support Systems Workshop, Cambridge, Mass., Ziff Institute, 1993.

6 Gery, Gloria J., Designing Electronic Performance Support Systems Workshop, Cambridge, Mass., Ziff Institute, 1993.

7 Quoted in Galagan, Patricia. "The Instructional Designer in a New Age," *Training and Development*, March 1994.

8 Gery, Gloria J., Designing Electronic Performance Support Systems Workshop, Cambridge, Mass., Ziff Institute, 1993.

9 Horn, Robert E., *Strategies for Developing High-Performance Documentation*, Waltham, Mass., Information Mapping, 1990.

10 Whiteside, Mary F., and Whiteside, Alan J., "Design Considerations for Implementing Hypertext in an Interactive Performance Support System," *Journal of Interactive Instruction Development*, Winter 1993.

11 Marotta, Robert E., ed., *The Digital Dictionary: A Guide to Digital Equipment Corporation's Technical Terminology*, 2d ed., Digital Equipment Corporation, Maynard, Mass., 1986.

12 Gery, Gloria J., Designing Electronic Performance Support Systems Workshop, Cambridge, Mass., Ziff Institute, 1993.

Choosing EPSS as the Performance Solution

THIS CHAPTER defines EPSS and conventional training and how to choose between the two approaches. It also describes performance situations where EPSS is the appropriate approach.

Comparing Training and EPSS

EPSS and conventional training can peacefully co-exist in the workplace.

Technological advances and challenges in the workplace are creating a need for electronic performance support. Some training experts believe that EPSS can replace conventional training. However, this book proposes that both approaches can peacefully coexist in the workplace (Figure 2-1).

Understanding each approach can help companies decide which is the appropriate strategy for enhancing employee performance.

Figure 2-1. Training and EPSS Are Complementary Approaches

Definition of Training

Training is a preplanned, goal-oriented approach to teaching people. Typically, instructional designers (IDs) create training in advance. IDs design training to help people acquire skills and knowledge prior to job task performance.

Training formats include:

- **Instructor-led**: lecture/lab, workshops, and seminars

- **Self-paced**: multimedia (video and audio), computer-based training (CBT), and print instruction

Definition of Electronic Performance Support

Electronic Performance Support Systems (EPSS) are self-contained, on-line environments that support job performance on an as-needed basis. Little to no human interaction is available or necessary. Support can be in many formats including those available in conventional training such as text-based, computer-based and multimedia instruction.

EPSSs typically provide support within the job context. The support and the job tasks are integrated, and the support is in the format that best matches the task.

Differences Between Training & Performance Support

People learn in a multitude of different ways. Some people like to attack a problem with a well-written manual. Others are too impatient to search for the answer and would rather consult with a coworker. Some people like the comfort of being taught by an expert in the given field at a training site that is far removed from the stress and strain of the worksite. Others want to "learn as they do."

Conventional training and EPSS differ in how and when they occur, how they relate to job tasks and the workplace, and how easily they adapt to performers and their work styles. Table 2-1 describes several differences between conventional training and electronic performance support.

Table 2-1. Comparing Training and EPSS

Factors for Comparison	Conventional Training	Electronic Performance Support
When does it occur?	Usually does not coincide with when the performers actually perform the work. Often occurs before or after performers really need the information.	Coincides with job task performance. Happens just as performers fulfill a task.
How is it connected to the workplace?	Usually is isolated from the performer's workplace. Occurs in an artificial environment such as a classroom or in computer-based simulation. Often, performers do not get to apply what they learn within the actual job context.	Is totally integrated into the performer's workplace. Support happens in context; performers request the information they need when they need it.
Does it adapt to performer differences?	Often does not adapt to differences. Training seeks to create "one message" for a homogenous audience rather than recognize that training audiences are heterogeneous and require "many messages."	Adapts to differences. Gives different messages to different people. Can support heterogeneous audiences, give high-level concepts, step-by-step instructions or decision support based on performer needs.
Does it accommodate different learning styles?	Sometimes cannot recognize differences in learning styles. Training is often focused on one learning style because of the expense and time required to tailor the training to different learning styles.	Recognizes differences in learning styles. For example, EPSS components let performers explore by browsing, learning sequentially or referring to electronic experts for guidance.

Factors for Comparison	Conventional Training	Electronic Performance Support
Is it flexible or static?	Training is static. Often cannot accommodate changes in information or processes because it is created in advance. Training takes a "snap-shot" of performance and delivers to that image.	Performance support is flexible. Accommodates changes in job task and can easily accommodate additional information.
Is it ongoing?	Is not ongoing. Training has a distinct beginning and end. Support is usually not available when the performer returns to the workplace.	Is ongoing. Is available when the performer needs it. Is built into the performer's computer system at the workplace.

Choosing the Right Approach

The work world of the 1990s places many demands on its workers. Information, technology, employer and industry expectations, and the work itself are increasingly more difficult to control. Training and performance support alternatives such as EPSS have a role in helping performers feel more in control and competent in the marketplace.

By looking at the trends and the demands of the workplace, employers can decide if the correct approach for their workplace is conventional training or EPSS.

EPSS may be a good solution under these circumstances.

When to Choose EPSS

EPSS is a good solution for enhancing performance when the following company, performance, or performer conditions are present.

Information and Technology Explosions Exist

The information and technology explosion are a blessing and a curse. Employers bombard their employees with so much information that it is hard to organize, read, and relate it to the job. Technology brings its own burdens. Cellular phones, laptop computers, pagers, and PC technology change daily.

With a well-designed EPSS, employers can help their workers remain current. An EPSS can create one focal point for information, and help performers synthesize the information with their job.

Table 2-2 describes instances where information and technology warrant the use of an EPSS.

Table 2-2. How EPSS Supports the Information and Technology Explosions

An Electronic Performance Support System:	
Organizes *information* that is...	Makes sense of *technology* when...
• Overwhelming	• There are many software tools needed to perform the job
• Error-laden	
• Constantly changing	• Productivity tools are difficult to learn
• Available in many different formats	• The job requires customized software support
• Difficult to find	

Experts Are Not Available

Many employers rely heavily on in-house experts. These are employees who are extremely skilled, have mastered the job, and may even create tools to improve the job. Novice workers look to these experts to troubleshoot and answer questions.

Several problems occur with this worker model. First, experts have trouble completing their work because they are helping novices. Second, experts may intimidate novices, and they may be afraid to ask questions. Therefore, they may use the wrong techniques to per-form their jobs. Third, experts may not be available to assist novices because of job turnover or because the job is extremely specialized.

In these cases, an EPSS can act as the expert. The best practices, methods, and techniques can exist within it for use by novices. Rresume writing , for example is a specialized skill that the creators of Microsoft Word have programmed into the Resume Wizard.

Expectations for Performers Are High

Expectations for workers in the global marketplace are extremely high and time for enhancing skills is at a premium. Many employers want instant   productivity   but   cannot   afford   to   release   their employees to attend training. Productivity software may exist, but performers do not have time to integrate it into their working styles and habits. Levels of management have disappeared, making employees more independent and accountable for their work, but with little support to make this feasible.

In addition, the work force is large, diverse and constantly shifting. Workers move from company to company without transferring skills to those they leave behind. Yet, employers demand a consistent level of performance.

EPSS helps performers be successful by giving consistent support as performers need it. The expertise resides in the software, not within the mind of a key performer. EPSSs respond to the needs and styles of a diverse and multicultural work force. Also, EPSSs provide the appropriate level of support for novice, intermediate and expert performers.

Learning Styles Suitable for EPSS

The EPSS concept is particularly useful for performers who prefer a self-directed style of learning.

When to Choose Training

Conventional training may be a good solution under these circumstances.

EPSS may *not* be a good solution in all instances. Conventional training in an appropriate format might be a better solution when the following company, performance, or performer conditions are present.

EPSS Development Resources Are Not Available

EPSS design and development require a specialized team of professionals. Some of the skills the team must have are software engineering, instructional design, graphic user interface design and so on. Building a team with these varied skills may not be possible, nor may there be the funding to support the EPSS development effort.

Insufficient Lead Time for EPSS Development

EPSS design and development require significant lead time. If the resources are unavailable and timelines are tight, conventional training may be a more appropriate approach.

Type of Instruction or Content Not Suitable

The job content or processes may not be appropriate for EPSS. The following are situations where training may be the more appropriate choice:

- Sequential or structured training is needed.
- Learning situation requires preliminary knowledge to achieve performance goals.
- Simple remediation, drill, or practice are appropriate.
- Standardized training is a requirement (the law dictates specific training requirements for certification).

Job Training Requires Human Interaction

Some professions require interaction between instructor and student or between groups of students. For example, firefighters who are learning cardiopulmonary resuscitation must learn this process in a classroom where there is one-on-one instruction using an inflatable dummy. Professions where conventional training may be more appropriate include jobs where performers:

- Must make split-second decisions in life-threatening or critical situations (knowledge and skills must be instinctual).
- Perform crisis counseling.
- Depend solely on interpersonal interaction.

Learner Styles Are Suitable for Training

Training may be more appropriate for performers who are less self-directed or want more external control over their training. Some learners need the discipline of classroom training to learn.

Choosing Formats When EPSS is the Approach

Descriptions, advantages, and constraints of EPSS media formats.

An EPSS can include many media formats including audio, video, computer-based training and interactive video instruction.

In 1992 Digital Equipment Corporation created a document called "*US Education and Training Instructional Design and Media Selection Guidelines.*" This document describes the advantages, constraints and quality standards of a number of media formats.

This document is a useful tool for deciding which formats to use *within* an EPSS.

The next section provides descriptions, advantages, constraints, and quality standards (condensed from the "Guidelines" document) for the following formats:[1]

- Audio
- Video
- Computer-based training

Audio

Information is presented through an audiotaped instructional sequence.

Advantages

- Can provide a model behavior to be emulated; for example, a sample presentation
- Can be distributed to a widely dispersed audience
- Inexpensive to reproduce

Constraints

- Requires a formal development and production process involving equipment and personnel
- Requires a manufacturing process
- Some people don't learn well with audio alone

Quality Standards

- Narrator is a professional
- Speed of narrative enables learning
- Audio quality is good
- Presentation is well structured and interesting

Video

Information is presented through a videotaped instructional sequence.

Advantages

- Provides opportunity to demonstrate skills
- Can be highly motivating
- Good for changing or shaping attitudes

- Delivers a consistent message to all students
- Can be easily distributed to a geographically dispersed audience
- Provides an opportunity to visualize/see at angles and magnifications that would otherwise be impossible

Constraints

- Requires stable content
- Need special equipment
- Expensive to develop
- Can be expensive to update or modify
- One-way channel of communication
- May become outdated

Quality Standards

- Narration and presentations are professionally done
- Presentation is well structured and interesting
- Full advantage is taken of the medium's unique characteristics
- Graphics add to the value of the presentation

Computer-Based Instruction

A computer program presents the information, examples, practice, and feedback to the students.

Advantages

- A very high degree of individualization is possible
- Potential exists for a high degree of learner control over pace and content
- Delivers a consistent message across groups of students
- Opportunities to review and practice are unlimited
- Immediate feedback on practices and tests
- Good for teaching knowledge and skills

Constraints

- Expensive to develop
- May require significant lead time for development
- Not good for teaching concepts or skills requiring human interaction
- Requires stable subject matter
- Requires a large number of prospective students to be cost-effective

Quality Standards

- Pace and content can be controlled by students
- Learners can repeat and review material
- Text and graphics are easy to read and understand
- Program is appealing and realistic
- Learners can pass over materials that are already known or not desired

Looking at EPSS Solutions

Electronic Performance Support Systems can improve performance in a wide variety of industries. EPSS can have an impact on a number of professions, from the sales to manufacturing. Table 2-3 describes some performance problems and EPSS solutions.

Table 2-3. Performance Problems and EPSS Solutions

Industry	Problem	EPSS Solution
Software Design	Software engineers cannot easily and quickly design software given the complex data relationships, large systems, and so on. *Consequence*: Poor software application quality, user dissatisfaction, unclear task requests.	• Programmer productivity software • User monitor system that provides support material • Advisor • Library of articles and software code • Interactive training and reference *Benefits*: Improved software quality.
Customer Service	Customer service clerks at a major waste management company cannot keep up with the billing system and customer record updates. *Consequence:* High staff turnover, inexperienced workers, dependence on help desk.	On-line customer service and billing system that includes: • Database • Help system *Benefits:* Fewer calls to the help desk and increased productivity.

Industry	Problem	EPSS Solution
Manufacturing	Operators at a computer chip manufacturing company rely on print documentation to check for chip defects. The documentation cannot reside on the manufacturing floor. *Consequence:* Operators lose time making trips between documentation and workstation and forget what chip defects look like.	On-line visual databases of: • Known chip defects • Defect-free chips • Audio coaching of chip conditions *Benefits:* Increased productivity, reduced time to discover defects, ability to easily add information to system.
Sales	Sales force at a major computer company cannot keep up with changing product lines and the information they use to sell products. *Consequence:* Productivity losses from placing sales reps in classrooms, expense of expert reps coaching novice reps.	Integrated sales environment consisting of: • Information database • Expert advisors • Learning experiences *Benefits:* Faster access to information, reduction in information overload.
Government	Personnel specialists need a standard approach for handling employee relations problems. *Consequence:* Specialists have to rely on high-paid employee relations consultants for guidance.	On-line system that encapsulates the expertise of employee relations group including: • Computer-based training • Expert system • Hypertext database *Benefits:* Substantial reduction of reliance on consultants.

1 Digital Equipment Corporation, US Education and Training Instructional Design and Media Selection Guidelines, 1992.

Justifying EPSS

THIS CHAPTER provides justification for investing in EPSS and assesses an organization's readiness for using EPSS as a performance enhancement strategy.

Justifying EPSS: An Overview

EPSS is part of the evolution of learning theory, practice and educational technology.

In the 1970s, a method for recording and playing music called "8-track" appeared. Americans rushed out and brought bulky 8-track players and cartridges, investing hundreds of dollars. Audio cassettes appeared, replacing 8-tracks.

In the 1980s, the video industry announced Beta technology. Video fanatics invested thousands of dollars in Beta-format video cassette recorders and video cassettes. VHS technology appeared, making Beta technology obsolete.

The education and training world has witnessed its own "technological evolution". Computer-based training (CBT) replaced printed programmed textbooks, and multimedia training threatens to replace CBT.

Why invest in EPSS? Is it a fad – a technology that is here today, but will be gone tomorrow? Is the investment worth the return? Does it *really* make good business sense?

This chapter demonstrates that EPSS is an *approach, not a technology*, that makes good business sense for companies.

Solving Business and Performer Needs

Technological advances, a shifting world economy and the overflow of information make for a challenging business environment. These and other changes in industry have resulted in business and personal needs that are best met by EPSS.

Business Needs

EPSS addresses performer competence, self-reliance and customer satisfaction.

Total quality management. Business process re-engineering. Self-managed teams. These are techniques that today's companies are using to create better products and services faster, increase quality, and cut costs. A key to the success of these techniques is the work force, the modern-day performer.

Companies need their employees to become competent faster and increase their efficiency and productivity. EPSS can make this happen.

EPSS can positively affect performance in the following ways:

- Decrease time to competency
- Increase performer competency
- Decentralize decision making
- Increase customer satisfaction

Decrease time to competency

EPSS decreases the 12 to 24 month new employee learning curve.

Employees in new job positions typically take *12 to 24 months* to become competent at their jobs. This means that it can take as long as two years for employees to work independently at appropriate productivity and quality levels. Employers typically provide training and on-the-job support (mentoring, coaching, job aids) during this period. This level of support is expensive and time-consuming. Note that this is bringing employees from "neophyte" to "competent," not from "neophyte" to "expert" performance levels.

Employers may never get the chance to reap the benefits of their investment in training and support. Malcolm recounts that in the field of life insurance, the industry average turnover rate for the sales force is 75% in the first 36 months. "If it takes a year and a half to develop a fully competent salesperson, and 75 percent of your new salespeople are gone within three years, that's a very expensive revolving door."[1]

EPSS can decrease the time to competency and make experts of neophytes. By providing expert advice, a neophyte can perform well above his or her current level of knowledge. A byproduct of having access to the knowledge of experts is that neophytes may increase their knowledge.

EPSS decreases task completion times.

Gery describes the decrease in time to competency for an EPSS she created. The task was a complex, error-ridden one that took an experienced employee 12 hours in the classroom to learn. With the EPSS, training time *decreased from 12 hours to 1 hour and 48 minutes,* and transaction time for the task *decreased from 17.1 minutes to 3.9 minutes.* These performers went from neophyte to expert in $\frac{1}{6}$ the time as the typical, experienced performer.[2]

This and other examples show that EPSS can be a valid approach to decreasing an employee's time-to-competency. See Chapter 2; *Choosing EPSS as the Performance Solution,* for more comparisons.

Increase Performer Competency

EPSS increases performer competence.

Companies not only want to decrease the time-to-competency curve, they also want more competent workers. There are two interrelated issues here; make performers more competent and make job processes more efficient.

Companies are looking for ways to make employees work smarter, faster, and better. Key to this goal is work redesign. As Malcom puts it, "Let's design the work, the processes and the systems together to seek order-to-magnitude improvements in productivity, not incremental change."[3]

EPSS supports or automates redesigned work processes.

Work redesign is integral to EPSS design. EPSS design looks at the performer *and* the work. During the Define phase, instructional designers analyze the job environment. The designer may see a work process that is inefficient. The designer may make recommendations for streamlining and improving the work processes. The EPSS then *supports or automates this new and improved way of working.* The result is employees and work processes that are more efficient and more productive.

Example of EPSS and work redesign.

An example at Digital Equipment Corporation is the Learning Services Workbench. This EPSS supports consultants who sell training, services, and support solutions to customers.

The Workbench automates the change request process. This process and its form document any changes in an agreed solution. Consultants around the world request the same change request information, but each geography uses a different process and format. The Workbench uses an automated template. The EPSS prompts the Consultants for information and fills in the form, thus streamlining and standardizing the process and the information.

Decentralize Decision Making

EPSS supports "flatter" organizations by providing decision making support.

Today's organizations are "flatter," that is, there are fewer levels of management, and more decision-making responsibility in the hands of lower-level workers. An article entitled "Performance Support: Worker Information Systems" describes this phenomenon and also makes a distressing observation: "Businesses...[are] pushing decision-making into the hands of more people – ones closer to the customer or the task. Yet people need help in doing these tasks."[4]

A well-designed EPSS supports this goal by:

- **Giving employees the resources to make decisions**
  EPSS can capture the knowledge and skills of experts (expert systems) and put that information at performers' fingertips. This helps performers make decisions.

  For example, an EPSS for a computer sales group could provide sales success stories, customized sales presentations, product and service information sheets, and advice on making the sale based on performer input.

- **Freeing employees from repetitive tasks**
  EPSS automates repetitive tasks and nonessential job tasks. This frees the employee to perform higher-level and "value-added" tasks.

  For example, an EPSS for an insurance adjuster could provide preformatted and automated forms to decrease the time adjusters spend filling out paperwork.

Increase Customer Satisfaction

An EPSS can create a positive cycle of supported employees, decreased costs, better products and increased customer satisfaction.

Performer Needs

EPSS addresses the needs of performers.

Performers have specific needs, concerns and motivations that are in addition to those expected by their managers, such as:

- Keep up with information
- Become more efficient and productive
- Increase autonomy and independence
- Increase motivation

Keep Up With Information

Imagine having an electronic "librarian" who sifts through the reams and reams and screens and screens of information that crosses each of our desks every day. This librarian does intelligent searches – selecting only the information that is relative to what we're currently doing. With EPSS, this is not a future dream, but a current reality.

The "information explosion" has brought an incredible array and amount of information into the hands of every worker. While it is great to have information, the sheer volume of information is over-whelming. Sifting through it to find out what applies to job tasks can be a full-time job.

An EPSS puts structure around information. An EPSS organizes the information and lets performers read and use just what they need to perform specific tasks.

Become More Efficient and Productive

EPSS experts describe how EPSS improves efficiency and productivity.

EPSS proponents recognize that employees want to work more efficiently and productively. Doing a good job is important in light of personal pride and manager's expectations.

Table 3-1 describes how EPSS supports efficiency and productivity goals as described by current experts in the field.

Table 3-1. How EPSS Increases Efficiency and Productivity

What the EPSS Does	What the Experts Say
Supports added-value, ancillary, and distracting tasks and automates or removes wasteful tasks	"Most jobs combine tasks that add value to the product, tasks that don't add value themselves but that are ancillary to tasks that do add value, tasks that must be performed but add value only indirectly and thus are distracting, and tasks that are simply wasteful."
	"Effective PSSs will support the first three types of duties in different ways. They won't support the fourth type at all."[5]
Internalizes best processes and practices	"Performance support spreads best practice as well as new procedures and insights through-out the organization."
	Performance Support: Worker Information Systems
Provides efficiency tools and templates	"Whenever possible, you are given samples, outlines, boilerplate, or templates...that the program attempts to customize."[6]

| Puts expert advice in the hands of the full range of workers – from novice to expert | "An advisor [expert] might suggest to a neophyte the most effective ways to perform specific tasks. When the performer is experienced, the advisor might help only with the most unusual situations."[7] |
| Gives easy access to information that workers had to memorize or know before | "Nowadays, many people – such as sales people of complex product lines – can't possibly memorize all of the information they need to do their jobs. Electronic performance-support systems can retain that necessary information for them."[8] |

Increase Autonomy and Independence

EPSS promotes self-reliance and decreases dependence on others.

EPSS gives performers the independence to make computer-assisted decisions. Typically when an employee begins a new job or learns a new task, there is a great deal of reliance on the "resident expert." The employee refers to this person for answers to questions as they arise.

This process can be inefficient. There may be delays as the employee waits for information, the "resident expert" may be unable to complete work because they're answering questions, or worse yet, the employee may be afraid to ask for advice and guesses the answer. This is incredibly dangerous in professions like banking or engineering where a wrong guess can mean a costly mistake.

The EPSS gives the performer the "best practice" – the preferred and most efficient way of performing tasks.

While the fear is that EPSS will replace employees, instead it assists them.

Increase Motivation

Because performing a task with support usually means performing a task well, EPSS can increase motivation. Each success can mean that an employee branches out to take on more work challenges with increased confidence.

Gaining a Competitive Advantage

The changing face of business makes EPSS an excellent option for supporting performers. Today's companies can use EPSS to capitalize on the following trends:

- Eighty percent of learning occurs on the job.
- More employees are telecommuting.

- Service industries are on the rise.
- The technology exists for EPSS.
- Conventional training is too costly.

Eighty Percent of Learning Occurs on the Job

EPSS supports performers on the job where most learning occurs.

EPSS is an appropriate option for learning based on certain statistics about *where and how* employees learn. Malcolm states that only a small percentage of employee skills are learned on the job: "a six-year study of managers at Honeywell Corp., completed in 1985, pegged the figure at about 20 percent."[9]

Not only are most skills *not* learned in training programs, but also the best methods by which employees learn do not match the methods that training programs use. Gery states, "Our [training] programs simply don't incorporate enough of the realities of how people learn...just compare the instructional strategies...in most formal training programs against the trial and error, inquiry, observation and behavior modeling, and coaching approaches described by learners as their primary and most effective learning strategies."[10] These methods are integral to EPSS.

More Employees Are Telecommuting

EPSS supports a current trend – working at home, or *telecommuting*. More and more companies are providing the means – computer systems, software, modems, and data lines – to support telecommuters. Albright and Post point to the increase in employees who work from home. "about 5.5 million people telecommuted (worked from home) in 1991, according to researchers at Link Resources. That figure represented a 38 percent increase from 1990. If the trend continues, the use of electronic performance support is likely to boom, because it can allow workers to access the support they need, when they need it – and from any location with a compatible computer."[11]

Service Industries Are on the Rise

Service companies use EPSS as an alternative to classroom training.

Companies that traditionally are not considered service companies are increasing their services to give them the competitive edge. In addition, service industries are on the rise. EPSS supports service. "Service industries are on the rise, and performance support appropriately focuses on serving customers, sales support, life insurance policy design and other service tasks."[12]

EPSS is an attractive strategy for the service industries because these industries rely heavily on the skills of their people resources. Horn emphasizes that service industries typically use training to increase knowledge and skills. However, training takes service workers away from the job and this decreases the volume of service and the resulting revenue. Horn remarks that EPSS can solve this problem. "If employees don't have to spend as much time in trainng, then they are available more often to provide service. If they are given the tools or procedures which increase their efficiency and skills (and compensate when necessary for lack of training), the amount and quality of their service are further increased."[13]

The Technology Exists for EPSS

The technology exists today to support EPSS development. Hypertext, expert systems, personal computers, client/server technology and many other advances in software and hardware have helped advance the cause of EPSS.

Conventional Training Is Too Costly

Companies predict a decrease in classroom training and an increase in technology-based training.

Companies are looking for alternatives such as EPSS to replace costly classroom training. Panepinto quotes this statistic, "A recent survey of 512 companies found that more than 60% predicted they would increase use of interactive video, computer-based training or other digital training technologies over the next three years, while only 18% predicted an increase in classroom training. Part of the reason for the shift in emphasis is the high cost and non tailored nature of classroom training."[14]

While EPSS design and development costs may seem high, conventional classroom training has many hidden costs that can make it an even costlier option. In Table 3-3, Dublin compares the cost of EPSS and training based on training 500 employees on how to use a $10 million system. The comparisons assume a 12-month payback in a billion-dollar organization.[15]

Table 3-3. Cost Comparison of Training and EPSS

		Traditional Approach		IPSS Approach
Lost opportunity cost in the first year The cost incurred while staff waits to be trained.	Cost	$2,500,000 Traditional training occured over 12 months. Full payback could have been achieved in six months, but users had to be trained. Assume 50% of six month payment lost in the first year.	Cost	$0 System implemented in six months. Training on the job. No time lost.
Lost work time Time spent training means time lost from regular duties	Cost	$1,000,000 Average cost to employ one person is $1,000 per week (salary + equipment + benefits); If each of 500 employees gets two weeks of training, it costs the company.	Cost	$200,000 With IPSS, training lasts only two days.
Training expense What it costs for in-house training.	Cost	$475,000 Employing two trainers and setting up a facility to train 500 users in one year cost $375,000. Cost for developing two weeks' worth of courseware is $100,000.	Cost	$60,000 Cost for facilitator/ coach to help with initial system use.
User support (help desk) The cost to support end users after training.	Cost	$200,000 Need two full-time employees (system experts), facility and equipment.	Cost	$100,000
System Development		$0 Not applicable		$1,000,000
	Total	$4,170,000	Total	$1,360,000

Source: Lance E. Dublin "Learn While You Work," August 1993. Copyright ©1993 *Computerworld* , Vol. 27, No 35 by Computerworld, Inc., Framingham, MA 01701. Reprinted by permission from *Computerworld*.

Note that:
- Cost savings with an EPSS approach are $2.81 million a 65% saving in the first year.
- Materials developed for traditional approach are immediately consumed. EPSS materials are a reusable asset.

See Chapter 2; *Choosing EPSS as the Performance Solution,* for additional comparisons of EPSS and conventional training methods.

Analyzing the Benefits of EPSS

Investing in EPSS is an important decision that companies should make after careful planning. Companies that do not perform analysis achieve disappointing results. While spending in information technology has increased dramatically, the expected benefit – increased employee productivity – has not occurred as shown in Figure 3-1.[16] "Many companies spend up to half of their discretionary capital on information systems and services in the belief that this would lead to productivity gains or provide competitive edge."[17] Companies can avoid these types of results by careful planning, evaluation and analysis *prior* to implementing an EPSS. The next section describes an analysis process.

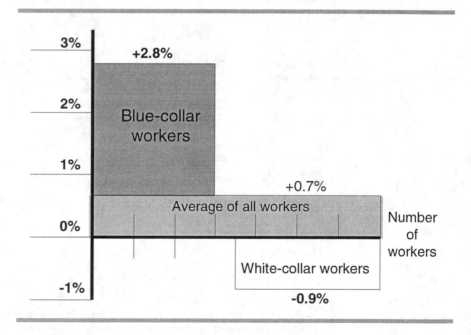

Figure 3-1. Private-sector Productivity Growth (1978–1985)

Conduct Cost, Benefit, and Risk Analyses

Cost, benefit and risk analyses are critical to EPSS decisions.

Companies should go through a process to weigh the costs, benefits and risks in implementing EPSS.[18] The steps in the process are:

1. Define the business environment.
2. Analyze the impact of EPSS.

3. Define the costs and benefits of EPSS.
4. Identify the risks of implementing EPSS.

Step 1. Define the Business Environment

Analyze strategic, financial technological and business activity.

In this step, the company should take a critical inward look. Analyze the business as it exists today from a strategic, financial, technological, and business activity standpoint. It is possible that this analysis could lead to business redesign prior to the EPSS design or to the realization that the company needs an intervention other than EPSS. An important part of this analysis is to look at cross-functional connections. For example, an EPSS for bank tellers affects the sales and accounting departments. The analysis helps the company look at positive and negative cross-functional impacts.

Critical Questions

Companies such as Digital Equipment Corporation use customized software to help companies analyze their business environment. Some critical questions that companies should consider are: [19]

- What are our strategic objectives?
- What is our financial picture?
- What is our budget?
- What is our technological picture?
- How will technology make it work?
- What is our system architecture?
- What are the current business trends?
- What are our short- and long-term goals?
- What are our constraints?
- What issues do we have?
- What obstacles do we face and how can we overcome them?
- What resistance will we encounter?
- What are our business activities and processes?
- What are critical functional interrelationships?
- How will we do business with the EPSS?
- How will people make it work?

See the section called *EPSS Readiness Checklist* in this chapter and Chapter 7; *ED⁴: The Define Phase,* for more on assessing the business environment.

Step 2. Analyze the Impact of EPSS

In looking at the business environment, the company should assess the impact that EPSS will have on individuals, groups and processes. This analysis can be performed manually or with customized analysis software. Figure 3-2 illustrates how looking at factors such as company objectives, technology, finances, and so on will affect the pre- and post-EPSS environment.

Figure 3-2. Analyzing the Impact of EPSS

Step 3. Define the Costs and Benefits of EPSS

Look at the costs and benefits of different EPSS development and delivery scenarios.

The impact of the EPSS can now be translated into costs and benefits. The company can calculate the costs and benefits of:

- Leasing versus buying
- Mixed-vendor versus single-vendor strategies
- Different hardware and software platform strategies
- Costs and benefits of different EPSS solutions
- Life cycle costs of an EPSS purchase
- Comparing outsourcing versus in-house EPSS development

Table 3-4 describes specific costs, benefits, and outputs that Digital Equipment Corporation produces using ProphIT, Digital's cash flow analysis tool.[20]

Table 3-4. Cost/Benefit Analysis

Cost Inputs	Benefit Inputs	Outputs
General information:	Estimated operating gains:	Analysis results:
– Length of evaluation period	− Equipment expenses eliminated	− After-tax net cash flow
– Tax rate	− Efficiency-related cost reductions	− Discounted cash flow
– Discount rate		− Payback period
		− Total costs

Hardware & software
depreciation:
- Economic life of assets
- Residual value
- Depreciation schedule

Assets purchase costs:
- System costs
- Peripheral costs
- Other hardware costs
- Software costs
- Financing costs

Leasing expenses:
- Payment schedule
- Lease duration

- Staffing costs
  displaced
- Productivity gains
- Effectiveness gains
- Innovation gains
- Equipment sale

- Net annual cash flow
- Cumulative cash flow

Cost Inputs	Benefit Inputs	Outputs

Upfront expenses:
- Personnel training, recruiting, planning
- Communications: lines, modems
- Facilities & expenses

Operating expenses:
- Hardware & software maintenance
- Personnel staffing, network management, training
- Network & communication lines
- Facilities & other expenses

Cost of Ownership

*Look at the cost
of the EPSS
throughout the
software's lifecycle.*

During cost/benefit analysis, the company should look at total costs. This includes anticipating the future. Companies, "...need to take a strategic view, forecast and plan for change. Information systems implemented to support specific requirements will not continue to deliver benefits as business changes."[21]

The Comprehensive Cost of Ownership (CCOO) model uncovers all the costs of information systems such as EPSS. [22] This is for the entire lifecyle of the EPSS including purchasing, owning, and operating a computer system, as well as growing with the performer's needs and the environment for many years.

The model in Table 3-5 uncovers all the costs of system owner-ship through the life cycle of:

- Acquisition and installation
- Operations and real maintenance
- Expansion and incremental change

Table 3-5. Comprehensive Cost of Ownership (CCOO)

Costs	Acquisition	Operation	Incremental Change
❶Hardware	Hardware equipment purchase Installation costs	Maintenance warranty Annual lease/rental charges	Hardware replace-ment or upgrade Deaquisition costs Depreciation recapture
❷Software	Software purchase/one time license Initial charge	Annual license fees Software maintenance fees Warranty	Software upgrades or replacement fees
❷Personnel	Recruiting Training/education Planning, design and selection Hardware and Soft-ware installations Contract programming	Routine monitoring and operations Problem determination and correction User liaison and administration Programming maintenance Contract programming	User charges Software changes and upgrades Training/education Programming Contract programming
❸Communications Carriers	Initial hook-up charges	Monthly tariff charges	Additional lines and hook-up charges Tariff charges
❸Facilities	Facilities development Wiring costs Plumbing	Space expense Power consumption Air cooling	Incremental wiring costs Incremental space expense

❶ Costs only incurred if new hardware is required to support the EPSS.

❷ Costs incurred that are directly related to EPSS. Personnel costs will vary depending on the support required and the mainte-nance and upgrade desired.

❸ Existing costs that are not directly related to the EPSS.

Step 4. Identify the Risks of Implementing EPSS

*Identify the
risks in under-
taking a software
development effort.*

Any software development effort involves risk. Risk management is the process of identifying potential risks that may impact cost, time, quality, and scope. Careful analysis can result in strategies to avoid or reduce risks.

Digital Equipment Corporation recommends the process in Table 3-6 for managing risk[23].

Table 3-6. Risk Management Process

Risk Step	Action
Risk identification	• Identify risk factors.
Risk assessment and prioritization	• Assess the likelihood of each risk event occurring.
	• Evaluate the potential impact of each risk.
Risk reduction and contingency planning	• Identify and determine costs for actions that will minimize or eliminate higher-priority risks.
	• Assess which actions are cost-effective and will be taken to avoid or reduce risk.
	• Assigns actions to appropriate people.
	• Develop risk contingency plans. These plans document actions and associated costs to recover if risk events do occur.
Risk monitoring	• Monitor the effectiveness of risk reduction and contingency planning actions.

Common Risk Factors

The company can anticipate and plan for risks. For example, an EPSS team may decide to use multiple software platforms. The team may consciously decide to use an expert authoring software language to create a coach component and a hypertext authoring language to create reference information. These choices create certain risks:

- Working with third-party software: Are the software manufacturers reputable? Will they provide support? Will the software work within the hardware and software environment?

- Integrating the hypertext and expert system components: Will there be integration problems? Can these two components be integrated?

- Technical expertise of team: Does the team have experience with these two authoring environments? Can the software manufacturers answer the team's technical questions?

The following are generic risks for software development:

Component-Related Risk

The team assesses each component within the EPSS (coach, reference, data, and so on) and pinpoints risk. Types of risk are as follows:

- *Technical risk.* Identify this type of risk by assessing the following factors regarding the EPSS, technology and the EPSS development team:

  - EPSS complexity
  - Technical complexity of the team
  - Performance or functionality wanted
  - Integration issues
  - Possible product performance pitfalls
  - Maturity level of the EPSS technologies used (for example, hypertext, expert system, CBT, multimedia)

- *Third-party risk.* Identify this risk by assessing the following factors regarding any third-party software packages that the team uses to create the EPSS:

  - Financial viability
  - Run time finances
  - Product life expectancy
  - Previous experience
  - Experiences in similar development efforts
  - Company longevity
  - Willingness to work closely with the EPSS development team

- *Support risk.* Identify this type of risk by assessing the following factors regarding the EPSS development team:

  - Ongoing support availability
  - Competence of support engineers
  - Long-term availability of support engineers
  - Ongoing commitment to meet customer requirements
  - Ability of support engineers to make EPSS evolve with the performer environment

- *Business risk.* Identify this type of risk by assessing the following factors regarding the EPSS planning process and development team availability:

  - Completeness of requirements and functional specifications
  - Extent to which specifications match customer expectations
  - The impact of externally imposed decisions (product, development or deadline)
  - The extent of possible scope changes
  - The size of the software project (effort, duration, number of subprojects)
  - The size of the extended EPSS development team
  - Timely availability of key team members

- *EPSS-specific risk.* Identify this type of risk by assessing the following regarding EPSS environment and performer work environment:

  - The future directions of the EPSS concept (wireless and handheld technology, and so on)
  - Completeness of performance assessment
  - Changes in job/task environment
  - Changes in performer group or ancillary performer environments

Other Risks

- The customer regulatory environment
- Customer ownership or management
- Key customer, team, or subcontractor personnel
- Industry or economy
- Customer financial performance

Risk Reduction and Contingency Planning Strategies

Evaluate methods for reducing or eliminating risk before and during software development.

Once the team identifies the risks, the team must attempt to reduce risk or plan for contingencies. These strategies minimize the likelihood of a risk factor happening or create a cost-effective plan if a risk factor does occur.

Table 3-7 provides general risk reduction and contingency planning techniques.

Table 3-7. Risk Reduction and Contingency Planning Strategies

Risk Reduction Strategies	Contingency Planning Strategies

Reduce uncertainties about given risks:
 	
  — Prototype or model the EPSS
 	
  — Perform more detailed estimating, budgeting and scheduling
 	
  — Check references of third-party software manufacturers
 	
  — Ensure that EPSS team is adequately trained
 	
  — Rely on proven technology
 	
Reduce the consequences of a risk:
 	
  — Develop a parallel alternative solution
 	
  — Reduce the dependency of one EPSS component on another
 	
Avoid the risk:
 	
  — Reduce requirements or define them more completely
 	
  — Adjust time, scope, cost or quality as appropriate
	Use extra hardware, software or services from reputable third-party providers
	
	Identify and research new third-party providers
	
	Rework or redesign
	
	Increase resources
	
	Extend the schedule
	
	Reduce the scope
	
	Change quality standards

Assessing Readiness For EPSS

Assess a company's readiness for investing in the EPSS concept and technology.

Besides cost, benefit, and risk analyses, there is a "readiness" for EPSS that is not as easy to analyze. Decision makers may be hesitant or even resistant to introducing an advanced technological intervention such as EPSS.

Overcoming this resistance or hesitancy can be as simple as allaying some common fears that companies may have.

You *Can* Get There From Here

Companies may be concerned that they are not ready for EPSS, that they do not have the appropriate technology, or that they do not do the kind of work that's appropriate for EPSS.

The following are some of the common reservations and questions, as well as appropriate responses:

- **I've already made a significant investment in training.**
  EPSS can build on investments that companies have made in computer-based video and audio training. EPSS implementations can incorporate this kind of training.

- **I'm not comfortable investing in a large system.**
  Companies do not have to start out with a complex EPSS. A company can start small and grow. For example, the company can build a knowledge base that provides a specific group with hypertext information. Small EPSS investments can equal large performance gains.

- **My company's work is not conducive to EPSS.**
  Any field or industry – sales, manufacturing, high-tech – can benefit from EPSS. Companies around the country in these and many other fields have implemented successful EPSSs.

- **I don't know which group would benefit from EPSS.**
  Any group of employees that need support on the job can benefit from EPSS. However, Gery recommends this way to start. "Most consultants who build the systems recommend that companies begin with computer-related "knowledge jobs" in which people are following certain routine procedures. "Bank tellers are good candidates, for instance, as are many kinds of customer-service workers."[24]

- **We don't have PC software or hardware.**
  EPSS does not depend on PC technology, or a specific software or hardware environment, for that matter. EPSS can be created on many systems including mainframe systems such as VMS systems, OS/2, on so on.

EPSS Readiness Checklist

Readiness checklist: factors that signal that a company should consider EPSS as a performance improvement strategy.

Ladd created the following checklist to help organizations assess whether they are good candidates for EPSS. This checklist includes company and employee concerns and situations that are beyond the range of financial or technological readiness. It can be used in addition to the financial analysis recommended earlier in this chapter. Organizations should also refer to Chapter 2; *Choosing EPSS as the Performance Solution,* to decide if EPSS is the correct approach versus a training intervention.

According to Ladd, an organization is a good candidate for EPSS if it checks three or more items in the first section or four or more items in the second section.[25]

Section 1: Internal Pressures and Situations

- ❏ The training budget is being cut.
- ❏ The organization is downsizing.
- ❏ Employees have received a corporate mandate to improve quality.
- ❏ The company is committed to improving productivity.
- ❏ The company is deploying a large-scale new-business activity or rolling out new software.
- ❏ Employees work in different geographic locations.
- ❏ Employees use computers to do their jobs or they have access to computers.
- ❏ There is a high turnover rate.

Section 2: Employee Needs and Descriptions

- ❏ Varied skill levels are required to perform job-related tasks.
- ❏ Employees have diverse learning styles.
- ❏ Employees perform a variety of tasks that require training or support.
- ❏ To do their jobs, employees need access to experts.
- ❏ Senior managers consider the training and support of employees in job-related tasks important.
- ❏ Training must be divided into separate modules for each skill being taught.
- ❏ After training ends, employees can't remember all of the new information required to do their jobs.

- ❑ Employees are expected to learn while completing tasks.
- ❑ Job-specific information must be accessible during the perform-ance of tasks.

---

1 Malcolm, Stanley E. "Reengineering Corporate Training," *Training*, August 1992.

2 Gery, Gloria J., Designing Electronic Performance Support Systems Workshop, Cam-bridge, Mass., Ziff Institute, 1993.

3 Malcolm, Stanley E. "Reengineering Corporate Training," *Training*, August 1992.

4 EDventure Holdings, Inc. "Performance Support: Worker Information Systems," Re-lease 1.0, vol. 93, no. 8, August 1993.

5 Carr, Clay, "PSS! Help When You Need It, ," *Training & Development*, June 1992.

6 Jan Diamondstone The Workplace as Upstairs, Downstairs

7 Ladd, Carolyn, "Should Performance Support Be in Your Computer?," *Training & Development*, August 1993.

8 Carr, Clay, "PSS! Help When You Need It, ," *Training & Development*, June 1992.

9 Malcolm, Stanley E., "Reengineering Corporate Training," *Training*, August 1992.

10 Gery, Gloria J., "Training vs. Performance Support: Inadequate Training Is Now In-sufficient," *Performance Improvement Quarterly*, vol. 2, no. 3, 1989.

11 Albright, Robert C. and Post, Paul E., "The Challenges of Electronic Learning," *Train-ing & Development*, August 1993.

12 EDventure Holdings, Inc., "Performance Support: Worker Information Systems," *Release 1.0*, vol. 93, no. 8, August 1993.

13 Horn, Richard, "The Economic Advantage of Knowledge Support Systems," *Perform-ance Improvement Quarterly*, vol. 2, no. 3, 1989.

14 Panepinto, Joe, "Delivering Training," *Computerworld*, vol. 27, no. 45, November 1993.

15 Dublin, Lance E., "Learn While You Work," *Computerworld*, vol. 27, no. 35, August 1993.

16 Managing the Benefits of Information Technology Investments Seminar Sloan School of
Management Seminar, Zurich, November 29, 1993.

17 Digital Equipment Corporation. "Digital Consulting Services: Managing the Benefits of
Information Technology," Digital Consulting Services Information Sheet, Maynard, Mass., 1993.

18 Digital Equipment Corporation. *Investment Evaluation Methodology* , Maynard, Mass., 1993.

19 Digital Equipment Corporation. Managing the Benefits of Information Technology Investments, Seminar, November 29, 1993, Zurich.

20 Digital Equipment Corporation. Managing the Benefits of Information Technology Investments, Seminar, November 29, 1993, Zurich.

21 Digital Equipment Corporation. Digital Consulting Services: Managing the Benefits of Information Technology, Digital Consulting Services Information Sheet, Maynard, Mass., 1993.

22 Digital Equipment Corporation. *Comprehensive Cost of Ownership (CCOO) Quick Reference Guide*, Geneva, Switzerland, 1990.

23 Digital Equipment Corporation. Digital Program Methodology Techniques: Risk Management, Part no. EF-B6505-50, Rev. A, October 1992.

24 Geber, Beverly, "Help! The Rise of Performance Support Systems," *Training* December 1991.

25 Ladd, Carolyn, "Should Performance Support Be in Your Computer?," *Training & Development*, August 1993.

Prepare for EPSS Design and Development

2 PART

Chapter 4

Building an EPSS Development Team

THIS CHAPTER describes how to create the diverse group of professionals needed to create EPSS. This chapter also identifies the skills and knowledge needed to create a successful EPSS and training opportunities for the EPSS team.

A Diverse Team

The EPSS team consists of experts from various fields.

EPSS development provides the rare opportunity to combine the skills, knowledge, and talents of experts in various fields into a powerful development team. The team merges the disciplines of systems design and development, instructional design, usability, and graphic design (see Figure 4-1).

The team's diversity can cause conflict as professionals from many different disciplines try to find common ground as they work toward a common goal. If managed correctly, this diversity *can* cause a creative exchange of ideas, skills, and approaches that will overcome conflicts and result in a well-rounded EPSS.

Figure 4-1 EPSS teams are diverse

Identifying Team Roles

EPSS complexity determines the number of team members and skills and knowledge needed.

The complexity of the EPSS determines the skills and knowledge that the EPSS team needs (see the *Identifying Skills and Knowledge* section later in this chapter). For example, an EPSS with customized multimedia capability requires instructional designers with this expertise or a multimedia expert.

The number of team members varies. Typically, an individual team member has the skills to fill more than one role. On large development teams, there may be one person per role. On small teams, a single person fills multiple roles. For example, a software engineer or instructional designer on a small team fills their own role *plus* the project manager role.

The roles in Table 4-1 are *major* roles; additional team roles that the EPSS development team may need are administrative support such as data entry specialists, project specialists, and other software professionals such as user interface designers. See the *EPSS Role Descriptions* section next for descriptions of these roles.

Table 4-1. Major Team Roles Required

EPSS Team Roles	EPSS Components				
	Knowledge Bases	Coaches	Help Systems	Tools	Instruction
Sponsor	✓	✓	✓	✓	✓
Client	✓	✓	✓	✓	✓
Performers	✓	✓	✓	✓	✓
Project manager	✓	✓	✓	✓	✓
Software engineer	✓	✓	✓	✓	✓
Instructional designer	✓	✓	✓		✓
Graphic designer				✓	✓
Usability expert	✓	✓	✓	✓	✓
Quality control expert	✓	✓	✓	✓	✓

EPSS Role Descriptions

Table 4-1 identifies the major EPSS roles. Note that while the sponsor, client, and performer are not actively developing the EPSS, they are critical members of the extended team.

The following are role descriptions.

Sponsor

Person or organization that authorizes EPSS development and provides the corporate, organizational, and political support that is essential for EPSS success.

The sponsor also ensures that the various people involved in development and implementation work together. Carr emphasizes, "A successful PSS may require a sponsor that can persuade different groups to work together...And [the EPSS] is more apt to succeed because of this broad sponsorship."[1]

Client

Provides overall financial and corporate control for the EPSS development. The project manager consults with the client throughout the EPSS design and development process. The client typically reviews and signs off on project plans, design specifications and, ultimately, the finished product. The client also authorizes any changes in the schedule and budget.

The sponsor and client may be the same person.

Performer

Participates throughout the design and development of the EPSS. In the Define and Design phases, the performer contributes an understanding of the work environment and specific job tasks. In the Develop phase, the performer tests and reviews the EPSS

Project Manager

Coordinates the project including scheduling, staffing, managing communication, and defining and standardizing the development process.

The instructional designer or software engineer may fill this role, thus playing a dual role in the design and development process.

Software Engineer

Creates the software program, provides tool support, builds, tests, debugs, and installs software kits. This includes integrating the software tools in the EPSS and integrating the EPSS into the performer's work environment. The number of software engineers on the project depends on EPSS complexity and the engineering expertise that
each brings to the team. The software engineer may also have user interface design expertise. If not, another team member must bring this critical expertise to the team

The software engineer may also fill the project manager role if the EPSS originates in an engineering group.

Instructional Designer (Performance Technologist)

Brings expertise in learning styles and information design and analysis to the team. The instructional designer performs performer needs and task analyses, testing, and evaluation. The instructional designer is also a key contributor to the system and user interface designs.

Instructional writers (course developers) may be on the team to write instructions and help and design the knowledge base on large teams. On small teams, the instructional designer performs this role.

Graphic Designer

Consults on the visual design of the user interface. The graphic designer also creates visual displays and illustrations within the EPSS.

Usability Expert

Participates in the design and development to ensure that the EPSS operates consistently and is easy to use.

The graphic designer, instructional designer, or software engineer may bring this expertise to the team, thus combining roles.

Quality Control Expert

Reviews EPSS at critical stages such as pilot testing, prototyping and final delivery to ensure that the EPSS is a quality, error-free product that is consistent, meets standards, and works properly.

Identifying Skills and Knowledge

EPSS team members should have certain skills and knowledge to be successful. Different team members should bring this expertise to the team as described in Table 4-2.

Table 4-2. Skills and Knowledge

Skill or Knowledge	Client, Sponsor	Project Manager	Software Engineer	Instructional Designer	Graphic Designer	Usability Expert
Team Skills						
Team player	H	C	C	C	C	C
Communications	C	C	C	C	C	C
Negotiations	C	C	H `	H	H	C
Problem solving	H	C	C	C	H	H
Ability to work under pressure	N	C	C	C	C	C
Ability to meet deadlines	N	C	C	C	C	H
Commitment to quality	N	C	C	C	C	C
Creative	H	C	H	C	C	C
Analytical	H	C	C	C	N	H
Commitment to the EPSS concept	C	C	C	C	C	C
Commitment to team synergy	H	C	C	C	C	H
Flexibility	C	C	C	C	C	C
Ability to take critique	N	C	C	C	C	H
Independent worker	N	C	C	C	C	C
Ability to learn quickly	N	C	C	C	H	C
Ability to create large volumes of work in short time	N	N	C	C	C	H
Assertive	C	C	C	C	C	C
Detail oriented	N	C	C	C	C	C

Skill or Knowledge	Client, Sponsor	Project Manager	Software Engineer	Instructional Designer	Graphic Designer	Usability Expert
Team Skills						
Concise, clear, coherent writing skills	N	H	H	C	H	H
Ability to adhere to templates and standards	N	C	C	C	C	C
Knowledge of performer environment and job tasks	C	C	C	C	H	C
Ability to keep performer perspective	C	C	C	C	H	C
Understanding of business needs	C	C	H	H	N	N
EPSS Development						
Software design	H	C	C	H	N	H
User interface design	N	H	H	H	H	C
Instructional design	N	H	N	C	N	H
Course development	N	H	N	C	N	N
Expert system design	N	N	C	H	N	H
Database design	N	H	C	H	N	H
Software testing and debugging	N	H	C	H	N	H
Technical knowledge: software tools, systems, computer programming	H	H	C	H	H	H

Skill or Knowledge	Client, Sponsor	Project Manager	Software Engineer	Instructional Designer	Graphic Designer	Usability Expert
EPSS development						
Knowledge of current and future technological environments	H	C	C	C	N	C
Relationships with technical staff and software vendors	N	C	C	N	N	N
Knowledge of software reproduction, distribution, packaging	N	C	H	H	N	N
Project scheduling	H	C	C	H	H	N
Project budgeting	C	C	H	H	N	N

Legend: C = Critical, H = Helpful, N = Not Needed.

Identifying EPSS Team Training

The EPSS team must be creative about training.

EPSS is a new concept, and so training and support for EPSS design and development are scarce. In addition, EPSS development is so specialized that standard EPSS training that *does* exist (conferences and workshops) may not fit the needs of the team.

The project manager *must* be creative about identifying training and support opportunities for the team.

If formal training opportunities are not available, the project manager can work with the instructional designer to create specialized, informal training such as mini-workshops on selected topics or processes. For example, the instructional designer can create a workshop on EPSS design storyboarding.

Formal EPSS Training

Formal training consists of conferences, workshops, books and experts.

Training opportunities that *currently exist* include:[2]

- Conferences
- Workshops
- Books and articles
- Consultants
- Exposure

Conferences

Table 4-3 lists the conferences that exist for EPSS and EPSS-related subjects:

Table 4-3. EPSS Conferences

Conference	Sponsor
Computer Training & Support	Softbank Cambridge, Massachusetts 1-800-34-TRAIN
Interactive Multimedia	Society for Applied Technology (SALT) 703-347-0055
International Society for Performance & Instruction (ISPI)	ISPI Washington, D.C. 202-408-7969
Interactive	Ziff Institute Cambridge, Massachusetts 1-800-34-TRAIN

Workshops

Ziff Institute in Cambridge, Massachusetts, sponsors workshops specifically on EPSS, led by Gloria Gery. Gery is an internationally known expert on EPSS and the author of the book *Electronic Performance Support Systems: How and Why to Remake the Workplace Through the Strategic Application of Technology*.[3]

Call 1-800-34-TRAIN for workshop schedule, locations, and cost.

Books and Articles

Currently, there is only one book on the market other than this one that deals with EPSS. *Electronic Performance Support Systems: How and Why to Remake the Workplace Through the Strategic Application of Technology* (1991) by Gloria Gery is an excellent overview of EPSS including its evolution, definition, and case study examples.[4]

Excellent articles on EPSS and EPSS components are also available.

Consultants

Various companies nationwide are developing EPSS. These companies provide a wide range of services from consultancies to full-service EPSS development.

Exposure

Designers who are new to EPSS can gain a better understanding of the concept by seeing examples of EPSS implementations. Excellent examples of EPSSs that the team can view at local software distributors include Microsoft Word for Windows, Microsoft Publisher, Microsoft Profit, and Quicken.

Informal EPSS Training

Informal training consists of mentoring and custom workshops.

The team can supplement existing opportunities with the following experiences.

Mentoring

Informal mentoring (the sharing of expertise) within the team enhances the development process. Knowledge of each profession's terminology, processes and constraints helps the team members increase awareness and expertise. For example, software engineers can explain technical issues to nontechnical team members. Instructional designers can explain information design, learning and motivation strategies to technical team members.

Customized Workshops

Experts on specific topics can create specialized workshops for team members. For example, software engineers can teach storyboarding and flowcharting fundamentals. Instructional designers can teach interviewing and observation techniques. Usability experts can teach a workshop on designing user interfaces with the performers in mind.

These workshops can supplement formal training opportunities. The team can also customize generic workshops for the EPSS development team's specific processes.

---

1 Carr, Clay. "Performance Support Systems: A New HORIZON for Expert Systems," *AI Expert,* (May 1992).

2 Gery, Gloria J. Designing Electronic Performance Support Systems Workshop, Cambridge, Mass., Ziff Institute, 1993.

3 Gery, Gloria J. *Electronic Performance Support Systems: How and why to remake the workplace through the strategic application of technology*, Boston, Weinparten, 1991.

4 Gery, Gloria J. *Electronic Performance Support Systems: How and why to remake the workplace through the strategic application of technology*, Boston, Weinparten, 1991.

Looking at

EPSS Technology

THIS CHAPTER overviews the software and hardware required to develop and deliver EPSS and technological issues relative to both development and delivery environments.

What's Behind the Scenes?

A Caveat

Technology is as fickle as teenage slang. What's "in" today can be "out" tomorrow. This chapter discusses current technology and the issues in defining, designing, developing, and delivering Electronic Performance Support Systems (EPSS).

Technology Behind the Scenes

Technology supports EPSS reference, help, instruction and coaches.

Chapter 1; *What Is Electronic Performance Support?*, described the types of responses that performers receive from the EPSS. For example, an insurance adjuster whose EPSS assists in filling out insurance claim forms may receive a preformatted electronic claim form, advice on how to fill out the form, and access to training about the claims adjustment process.

In Chapter 1, these responses were referred to as the *aspects* or components of the EPSS. Technology supports these EPSS components. For example, in the previous example, an expert system provides the advice (enhanced with hypertext information and hypermedia graphics, video and audio), and a computer-based training module provides the training.

Definitions of the Technology

Underlying technology are expert systems, hypertext, hypermedia, multimedia, and databases.

Distinctions between technologies blur as we move toward a society where audio, video, and graphic information are as commonplace as text.

With that in mind, the technology that supports EPSS includes:

- Expert systems
  Expert systems provide the electronic equivalent of the knowledge, procedures, decision-making skills, advice, short-cuts, hints, tips, and best methods and practices of a human expert. Bossinger and Milheim state, "Expert systems allow human expertise to be encoded into a knowledge base (Rasmus, 1989) that can provide the experience and advice of a human expert quickly and accurately without requiring face-to-face meetings."[1]

- **Hypertext**
  Hypertext is linked information that performers can access in the sequence and format that they need, and at the point of need. Stevens adds, "Hypertext allows associational access to *text*. This means that a hypertext system can allow access to information, training, and feedback to precisely the depth and in precisely the sequence most effective for the individual user.[2]

- **Hypermedia**
  Hypermedia is a further extension of hypertext. As with hypertext, performers have associational access to information, but this information is in a variety of media including video, audio, graphics, and animation.

- **Multimedia**
  Multimedia is a more general term for the video and graphic, still and motion images, and audio that can exist as stand-alone elements in the EPSS or linked as in hypermedia.

- **Databases**
  Databases for EPSS are information stores that reside on
  mainframes in client/server environments or on stand-alone
  systems. They allow storage and retrieval of multimedia
  and text.

EPSS Applications of the Technology

Table 5-1 describes common EPSS components and the technology
that could be "behind the scenes." Note that certain technologies like
multimedia (video, audio, graphics, and animation) can be anywhere
in the EPSS depending on the sophistication of the system and the
usefulness of these media elements for performer job tasks.

Table 5-1. EPSS Components and Supporting Technology

Component	Technology				
	Expert systems	Hypertext	Hypermedia	Multimedia	Databases
Reference	✓	✓	✓	✓	✓
Help	✓	✓	✓	✓	✓
Instruction		✓	✓	✓	
Coaches	✓	✓	✓	✓	
Tools	✓				✓

The Development Environment

The environment to create an EPSS's underlying technology – expert
systems, hypertext, hypermedia, multimedia, and databases – consists
of:

- **Hardware**
  PCs and/or mainframe computers for development that simulate
  the delivery environment.

- **Software**
  Tools, authoring languages, and programming languages to
  create the components.

Hardware Platforms

EPSS can be developed on all major mainframe platforms and PC platforms.

Electronic Performance Support Systems exist on all major platforms, including the mainframe and PC environments listed in Table 5-2.

Table 5-2. Hardware Platforms

PC Environments	Mainframe Environments
Apple/Macintosh	IBM
IBM PC (MS-DOS based)	Digital Equipment Corporation
	Hewlett-Packard

While the software tools and the power of PC environments make development easier, creative EPSS designers can embed EPSS in mainframe computer applications. "You can even build performance support into a mainframe application, with the PS content displayed on a 3270 terminal. Obviously, it's hard to do so, and the result will never be as nice as fast-response, GUI client-server systems, but it is possible."[3] Bramer and Senbetta add, "An integrated system will not be dependent on any one particular platform, so organizations need not discard existing hardware."[4]

Hardware Needed

Low- or high-end hardware includes systems, hard drives, CD-ROM, and video and audio equipment.

Hardware requirements increase exponentially with the complexity of the EPSS. For example, a simple EPSS that provides hypertext information (text only) would not need the CD-ROM storage and retrieval required by an EPSS that provides hypertext information that is text, running video and complex graphics.

The following hardware requirements for low- to high-end systems are based on the work of D'Ignazio.[5]

Low-End System Requirements

A simple EPSS (for example, simple user interface and text-based hypertext) can be developed and run on:

- **Systems**
  Low-end MS-DOS PCs like MS DOS 80286 with floppy disks, or 2 MB 286 MS-DOS machines, or relatively inexpensive Macintosh PCs like the MAC Plus, MAC Classic, or MAC SE.

- **Hard drive or floppy drives**
  Can run on 2MB to 60MB hard drives or even two floppy disks.

High-End System Requirements

Complex EPSSs (for example, containing expert systems, multimedia, sophisticated user interfaces) require much more complex hardware.

- **Systems**
  DEC Alpha machine, Intel Pentium, and top-of-the-line Macintosh PCs like the Mac II and Quadra systems.

- **Hard Drives**
  Requires 20MB to 120MB hard drives.

- **CD-ROM**
  May require 600MB CD-ROM for storage and retrieval.

- **Video equipment**
  May include VCR, cables and adapters, video camera, videodisk player, video circuit boards.

- **Audio equipment**
  May include speakers, mixers, audio circuit boards, SCSI circuit cards and cables.

Software Platforms

Software platforms include CBT, hypertext and expert system authoring software.

Today's PC software manufacturers are creating software that is multi-functional. Either the functionality exists within the software to create many types of products or the links are there to incorporate information from other software. For example, Apple's HyperCard can create hypertext information as well as the rudimentary answer judging and branching that designers need to create modular learning experiences. Designers can use Microsoft Word for Windows to create the coding for hypertext , and Visual C can use the Word files to create the actual hypertext.

Other software is specialized for a particular product. For example, Instant Expert software specifically creates expert system, as opposed to a programming language like C++ that can create expert systems as well as the full range of software applications.

Single-Platform Development

Because of the vast array of software, and its multifunctional nature, Raybould recommends that developers choose either a combination of platforms or a primary development platform depending on the EPSS components that are being developed. There are benefits and limitations to each approach.[6] The following are some of the technologies from which to choose the platform, followed by descriptions of each technology:

- CBT authoring languages
- Hypertext/hypermedia
- Expert system software

CBT Authoring Languages

Computer-based training (CBT) authoring languages are powerful software packages that typically require developers to have minimal programming skills. Some CBT authoring languages include the full range of services from scripting and storyboarding to final kitbuilding. IconAuthor is an example of this type of authoring language.

Cook identified the major qualities that developers should look for in a CBT authoring language. This checklist has been modified and expanded for EPSS development.[7]

CBT Software Authoring Checklist

Does software allow the *developer* to:

Sophistication
- ❏ Create course map or pictorial representation of learning module?
- ❏ Create customized menus?
- ❏ Create a range of modules (simulations, hypertext, hypermedia, video, audio)

Programming ease
- ❏ Easily correct course maps via interactive debugging?
- ❏ Import programs created in other programming languages?
- ❏ Create animations and tutorials?

Information management
- ❏ Track performance (if needed)?
- ❏ Provide testing (if needed)?
- ❏ Manage and track information?

Graphics
- ❏ Create full-page graphics?
- ❏ Use graphics imported from other graphics software?
- ❏ Use a color monitor and printer?

Text creation
❏   Create hypertext?
❏   Import text from other text or word processing software?

Multimedia
❏   Edit existing videotape?
❏   Drive videotape, videodisk and audiotape players?
❏   Create a slide show?
❏   Master a videodisk?
❏   Access CD-ROM storage disks?

Does the software allow the *performer* to:

❏   Respond using a variety of methods?
      Examples: click "Y" for Yes or type Yes, select a multiple-choice let-
      ter or number
❏   Branch from topic to topic?
❏   Write notes in an electronic notebook?
❏   Record relevant parts of the module in an electronic notebook?

Hypertext/Hypermedia

Hypertext and hypermedia allow performers to explore information in their own way.

Geber believes that the creation of hypertext paved the way for EPSS. Geber points to the fact that hypertext tools can integrate EPSS components, permitting performers to, "follow their own streams of thought in searching for information."[8]

Hypertext authoring systems can include user interface design facilities, rudimentary response judging and, specifically, the ability to make connections between information. Hypermedia authoring systems add the ability to create audio, video and animation.

Stevens differentiates between hypertext and hypermedia as authoring environments: "Hypermedia systems allow creation of graphics, digital sound, and animation from within the development structure, in addition to text and data components. Hypertext allows access to and some manipulation of these components, but requires the developer to use other development tools for the initial generation of the components."[9]

Both hypertext and hypermedia authoring environments require interconnection with a programming language to develop the full range of EPSS components. While programming functions are built-in, they can be used to develop only very basic functionality. Park provides the examples that "HyperTalk" is a programming language for Macintosh's Hypercard system and "LISP" is used for the Xerox NoteCard system."[10]

Expert System Software

Expert system software includes a knowledge base, inference engine, and explanation facility.

Expert systems provide the knowledge, procedures, decision-making skills, advice, short-cuts, hints, tips and best methods and practices of human experts. According to Bossinger and Milheim, expert systems consist of three components: [11]

- *Knowledge base*: contains rules of thumb for solving problems.

- *Inference engine*: selects and uses appropriate information to reach conclusions.

- *Explanation facility*: interacts with user to get details of problem and provides suggestions or diagnoses.

Given these components, expert systems can be created using either of two methods:

1. Expert system shell
2. Programming languages

Method 1: Using an Expert System Shell

Expert system shells contain a built-in inference engine. The developers then add information to the knowledge base. While expert system shells typically include other tools to aid in the development process, these applications typically only address a narrow range of problems. Expert system shells are typically used for training and decision support purposes.[12]

Table 5-3 provides common expert system shells, prices, and the platforms they support.[13]

Table 5-3. Expert System Shells: Companies, Costs, and Platforms

	MS-DOS	Macintosh	Windows
EXSYS EL EXSYS Inc. 1720 Louisiana Blvd., N.E., Suite 312 Albuquerque, NM 87110 (505) 256-8356	✓		

	MS-DOS	Macintosh	Windows
1st Class HT AI Corporation 138 Technology Drive Waltham, MA 02254-9748 (617) 891-6500	✓		
Goldworks III Gold Hill, Inc. 26 Lansdowne Street Cambridge, MA 02139 (617) 621-3300			✓
Hyper X Millenium Software 1970 S. Coast Highway Laguna Beach, CA 92651 (714) 497-7439		✓	
Instant Expert Rush Order 3261 Ash Street Palo Alto, CA 94306-2240 (415) 494-8400		✓	
Level 5 Information Builders, Inc. 503 Fifth Avenue Indialantic, FL 32903 (407) 729-9046	✓	✓	
MacSMARTS Cognition Technology Corporation 1000 Massachusetts Avenue Cambridge, MA 02138 (617) 492-0246		✓	
Nexpert Object Neuron Data Corporation 156 University Avenue Palo Alto, CA 94301 (415) 321-4488	✓	✓	✓
VP-Expert WordTech Systems, Inc. 21 Altarinda Road Orinda, CA 94563 (510) 254-0900	✓		

	MS-DOS	Macintosh	Windows
Xi Plus Inference Corporation 550 N. Continental Blvd., 3rd Floor El Segundo, CA 90245-5052 (213) 322-0200	✓		

Note: The expert system shells identified in Table 5-3 are based on a survey conducted by Bossinger and Milheim. Five hundred surveys were sent to corporate and educational organizations creating expert systems. A list of organizations were obtained and approved by *PC AI Magazine*, and 137 surveys (27.4%) were returned and analyzed.

Method 2: Using Programming Languages

High-level programming languages such as LISP, PROLOG C, Microsoft Visual Basic, or object-oriented languages like C++ can produce the full range of expert systems. However, they require a computer programmer and a large development effort to create a good system. [14]

Graphical User Interface (GUI) Software

User interface builders are specialized software for creating GUIs.

While the ability to create user interfaces can exist within other software applications like hypertext and expert systems, there is software designed specifically for this purpose. Jacob describes three categories of user interface builders: [15]

- **Interface development tools (IDTs)**
  Graphic layout tools that let software developers create the basic user interface layout including attributes like size, color, and position. The IDT generates the C or user interface language (UIL) code that defines the interface.

  Examples: ICS Widget Databook, Integrated Computer Solutions' (ICS) Builder Xcessory

- **User Interface Management Systems (UIMs)**
  Includes the IDT and a means to link the interface and the software application (EPSS). Software developers can dynamically define, test and debug the interface.

  Examples: Visual Edge's UIM/X, Hewlett-Packard's Interface Architect

- **Dynamic Data Visualization Tools (DDVTs)**
  Environment for developing GUIs that allows changes to the design during run time.

  Example: Dataview

Multimedia Software

According to Semich, multimedia will become more of a mainstream medium in the very near future: "...multimedia is set to become increasingly important as a mainline data type built into most applications."[16] Some multimedia software includes powerful software development environments with interface creation and storage/retrieval capabilities. For example, GainMomentum software can be used to create "point and click" interfaces, text, graphics, video and audio, and the ability to retrieve data from databases. Semich identifies key multimedia software companies as described in Table 5-4. [17]

Table 5-4. Multimedia Development Tools, Companies and Platforms

Tool	Company	Platform
Authorware Professional	Macromedia Inc.	Windows NT, UNIX, Macintosh
Action!		
Director		
GainMomentum	Sybase	UNIX
IconAuthor	AimTech	Windows, UNIX, VMS, OS/2
Multimedia GRASP	Paul Mace Software, Inc.	
MEDIAscript	Network Technology Corp.	OS/2
Workplace/2	IBM	OS/2
Ultimedia Builder/2		

EPSS Development Software by Category

Table 5-5 provides a summary of the software that currently exists for hypertext, expert system, multimedia, object-oriented design (OOD) and CBT.

Table 5-5. Sampling of Software Used for EPSS Development

Software	Company	Hypertext	Expert Systems	Multi Media	OOD	CBT	GUI
Applescript	Apple						
Asymetrix ToolBook	Asymetrix Corporation						
C++							
Eager	Apple						
Frontier	Userland						
Gain Momentum	Sybase, Inc.			✓	✓	✓	
GUIDE	OWL International						
Hypercard	Apple Macintosh						
IconAuthor	AimTech Corp.						
Linkway	IBM	✓		✓			
Macromind Director	Macromedia	✓		✓		✓	
PowerBuilder							
SalesBUILDER	Trilogy						
Visual BASIC		✓		✓	✓	✓	

Multiple Platform Development

Multiple platform development refers to authoring the EPSS using more than one authoring language.

Raybould recommends choosing a primary development platform or developing a combination of platforms (multiple platform development). [18]

In multiple platform development, developers create EPSS components from a variety of technologies including:

- Text management and retrieval
- Computer-based reference
- Hypertext
- Electronic documentation
- Expert system shells

- Knowledge processors
- CBT authoring languages

Advantages and Disadvantages

The major advantages of multiple platform development are the power of using software specifically geared to a particular EPSS component and the reduced development times and costs associated with using specialized software.

The major disadvantage is integrating the EPSS components across different platforms and network environments.

Strategies for Multiple Platform Development

Strategies for successful multiple platform authoring for EPSS development.

Smith gives the following strategies for multiple platform CBT development that are applicable to EPSS development. The following section and Table 5-6 are based on Smith's research and experience[19]:

- **Use authoring software that provides porting tools**
  Porting tools make cross-platform development easier. Scalable and mappable fonts are an example of porting tools.

- **Use authoring software companies who provide excellent technical support**
  Use the following criteria to judge the expertise of the technical support staff:

  - Does the technical staff port across platforms?
  - Does the support staff know the hardware and software issues for your platforms?
  - Does the company have a user group or forum on a public access network such as CompuServe?
  - Is there a charge for technical support? If so, how much is it?

- **Create a test script and test it on every delivery platform**
  Create a prototype that includes all major requirements and test on the exact hardware and software configuration on which the team will develop and deliver

- **Plan for the additional expense relative to multiple platforms**
  The following are some of the additional costs to plan for:

  - Extra hardware and software
  - Licensing and run time fees for each platform

- Additional fees (maintenance, distribution, and training)
- Development experts for each platform
- Extra time for testing
- Extra design and programming costs
- Diminished functionality across platforms

Table 5-6 describes additional issues and solutions for multiple platform development and delivery.

Table 5-6. Issues in Cross-Platform CBT Development and Delivery

Potential Issues	Solutions
Filenames change across platform.	Name files using DOS conventions as this is the lowest common denominator.
Graphics look and perform differently across platforms.	Obtain and test sample graphic files from the authoring software company.
	Create a library of reusable graphics.
CBT must run in color and black and white.	Use a limited palette of colors.
	Test graphics in black and white.
	Use color sparingly.
Text fonts are different across platforms	Map or scale fonts.
	Use custom fonts.
	Change text to bitmaps.
	Use simple fonts and limited number of fonts.
Computer memory varies across platforms.	Keep track of memory allocation and deallocation.

The Delivery Environment

EPSSs can be delivered within a variety of different environments. Development strategies and respective issues for each environment are complicated and beyond the scope of this book.

This section introduces a variety of different delivery environments.

Types of Delivery Environments

Delivery environments include:

- PC Client/Server Network
- Stand-alone PC or PC Network
- Mainframe
- Portable

PC Client/Server Network

Client/server environments consist of PCs (clients) linked by workstations that serve as data servers and mainframe computers for data storage. Boch describes the relationships within the client/server environment as "cooperative processing." "The very nature of client/server applications suggests a form of cooperative processing, wherein the responsibility for carrying out the system's function is distributed among various nearly independent computational components that exist as part of an open system."[20]

An EPSS in a client server/environment could run word processing software and spreadsheets on the desktop PC, and the knowledge base of hypertext that serves those tools could reside on the mainframe.

Stand-alone PC or PC Network

An EPSS can reside solely on a single, stand-alone PC or on a number of networked PCs.

Some of the delivery issues to consider are:

- **Stand-alone PC**

  — Does the PC have the memory and storage to support the EPSS and the work applications?

  — Does the performer understand system backup procedures for the information the EPSS generates?

  — Who will be responsible for installing and upgrading the EPSS?

— How does a performer in another work group receive access to the EPSS?

- **PC Network**
  — Will the EPSS reside on one, several, or all PCs?

  — What mechanisms will the EPSS use to share information between performers?

  — Will performers share information?

  — What protection (if any) will reside on the network to protect EPSS information?

Mainframe

An EPSS can reside on a mainframe. While an EPSS on a mainframe might not have the more intricate user interfaces that PC EPSSs would have, it would still serve the major purpose of integrating work task and support.

Portability

The work culture of the 1990s includes a growing number of employees who have portable offices. The mainstays of these employees are portable devices such as cellular phones, pagers, and laptop computers. Supporting job tasks is essential for these environments as well.

EPSSs on laptop computers can be:

- **Occasional connect (wired)**
  The performer is not connected to a network for the majority of the time. When connected, the performer can submit, request or receive information from the mainframe.

  For example, one of Digital Equipment Corporation's EPSSs called Sales Horizon is geared strictly to sales representatives who work on laptops. Software, called the Delivery Manager, lets sales representatives request customer information from the network, disconnect, then reconnect later and retrieve this information.

- **Network reliant (wired)**
  The performer's laptop is only viewed as being "on the network" – receiving the services of the network – when the laptop is connected.

- **Wireless**
  Wireless technology removes the cables that connect devices – laptops, handheld computers, and printers – to a mainframe computer. Employees have access to their computer systems and colleagues from any location.

---

1 Bossinger, June, and Milheim, William D. "The Development and Application of Expert Systems: A National Survey," *Educational Technology*, July 1993.

2 Stevens, George H. "Applying Hypermedia for Performance Improvement," *Performance & Instruction*, July 1989.

3 EDventure Holdings, Inc., "Tools of the Trade," vol. 93, n. 8, August 24, 1993.

4 Bramer, William L.,and Senbetta, Ghenno. "The New Wave of Performance Support," *Chief Information Officer Journal*, September/October 1993.

5 D'Ignazio, Fred. "Getting a Jump on the Future," *Electronic Learning*, November/December 1992.

6 Raybould, Barry. "An EPSS Study: Prime Computer," Ariel PSS Corporation, Mountain View, CA, 1991.

7 Cook, E.K. "The Use of Macintosh Authoring Languages in Effective Computer-Assisted
Instruction," *The Journal of Recreational Mathematics*, vol. 21, no. 3, 1989.

8 Geber, Beverly. "Help! The Rise of Performance Support Systems," *Training*, December 1991.

9Stevens, George H. "Applying Hypermedia for Performance Improvement," *Performance & Instruction*, (July 1989).

10Park, Ok-choon. "Hypermedia: Functional Features and Research Issues," *Educational Technology*, (August 1991).

11 Bossinger, June, and Milheim, William D. "The Development and Application of Expert
Systems: A National Survey," *Educational Technology*, July 1993.

12 Bossinger, June, and Milheim, William D. "The Development and Application of Expert Systems: A National Survey," *Educational Technology*, July 1993.

13 Bossinger, June, and Milheim, William D. "The Development and Application of Expert Systems: A National Survey," *Educational Technology*, July 1993.

14 Bossinger, June, and Milheim, William D. "The Development and Application of Expert Systems: A National Survey," *Educational Technology*, July 1993.

15 Jacob, Paula, "Beyond the GUI Gridlock," *HP Professional*, May 1993.

16 Semich, J. William, "Multimedia Tools Are Enterprise Ready," *Datamation*, October 15, 1993.

17 Semich, J. William, "Multimedia Tools Are Enterprise Ready," *Datamation*, October 15, 1993.

18 Raybould, 1993.

19 Smith, Sarah, "Cross-Platform CBT Development," *CBT Directions*, January/February 1993.

20 Boch, Grady. *Object-Oriented Analysis and Design With Applications*, Redwood City, Calif., Benjamin Cummings, 1994.

A Process for EPSS Design and Development

PART 3

ED⁴: A Design and Development Approach

THIS CHAPTER introduces ED⁴: a structured approach for defining, designing, developing, and delivering Electronic Performance Support Systems (EPSS).

Why Use a Structured Development Approach?

A Solution Looking for a Problem

Inadequate or non-existent planning results in an incorrect solution.

A field service manager for a computer company approaches a training manager. "I need a computer-based training course to teach my field service technicians how to troubleshoot our new printer," she says. The training manager organizes a team to create the course. With the new PC authoring tools currently available, the computer-based training (CBT) development team starts writing the course immediately. The team finishes the CBT in a month, and the training manager delivers the course to the field service manager.

Within a month, the field service manager returns to the training manager. "My technicians *still* can't troubleshoot the printer. Most of my technicians haven't even looked at the CBT, and those who have aren't any better at troubleshooting. I thought you said the CBT would solve the problem." The training manager looks baffled. "I thought the CBT would solve the problem too."

Why didn't the CBT solve the problem? The training manager did not ask some critical questions, nor did the team perform some critical activities. The result: a mismatch between the customer problem and the performance solution.

Situations such as this one can be avoided by using a structured development approach. A structured approach explores questions like:

These questions get answered with a structured approach.

- Who has a performance problem?
- What is the performance problem?
- What is the cause or causes?
- What is the proper solution?
- What is the plan to move from problem to solution?
- How do we keep the performer in the plan?

ED⁴: A Solution for Performance Problems

Experts in the fields of instructional design, software design, and performance technology recognize that there is a mismatch between training and performance solutions and problems. Fischer states, "a correct implementation with respect to a given specification is of little value if the specification is wrong to begin with and does not solve the given problem."[1]

Experts agree that using a structured approach can eliminate many of these mismatches.

Figure 6-1. ED⁴ (EPSS Define, Design, Develop, Deliver)

This book recommends that EPSS designers use ED⁴: Define, Design, Develop, and Deliver.

What is ED⁴?

*ED⁴ is
Define,
Design,
Develop,
and Deliver.*

ED⁴ is an instructional design and development methodology. ED⁴ stands for Define, Design, Develop, and Deliver (see Figure 6-1). Educational professionals can use the process to create any instructional products (computer-based instruction, lecture/lab, self-paced print instruction).

This book tailors ED⁴ to the specific needs of EPSS design and development. Table 6-1 describes each phase of the process, including phase descriptions and outcomes.

Table 6-1. ED⁴ Phases, Descriptions, and Outcomes

Phase	Description	Outcomes
Define	Determine the performance problem, create a profile of the performer, define the job and critical job tasks to be met by the EPSS, outline the technical functionality of the EPSS (including hardware and software strategy), identify master performers, define implementation strategy, define EPSS support and maintenance plan.	Performance assessment; Task assessment; Software application requirements; Project plan; Project schedule; Software functional; Specification; Support and maintenance plan
Design	Identify, collect and organize information, create tools, templates and standards, deter-mine and flowchart the EPSS component strategy, define hardware and software plat-forms, design the user inter-face, test the design strategy.	Information architecture; Software authoring strategy; Tools, templates and standards; Detailed design specification; User interface design
Develop	Create EPSS, integrate and test system, perform quality control, build software installation kit.	Prototype; Quality control approval; Software installation kit; Pre-implementation checklist
Deliver	Install and test EPSS, evaluate EPSS, implement support and maintenance strategy.	Software evaluation; Follow up plan; Project file; Post project review

Phase	Description	Outcomes
Project Management	Span the entire design and delivery cycle, and ensure quality, teaming, client interaction, and financial accountability.	Client communication plan; Quality control plan; Financial tracking; Team building

ED[4] Means Instructional and Systems Design

ED[4] incorporates good instructional and systems design.

Domain-oriented design, object-oriented design, knowledge support systems design, instructional systems design – these phrases are all examples of the exciting work that is currently taking place in the educational, performance technology, and systems design professions. And although each profession has its own unique thoughts, terminology, and methodologies, each contributes to good EPSS design.

The experts call for collaboration between the disciplines.

Instructional experts observe that good EPSS design involves the collaboration of instructional and systems experts. Wager states, "We [instructional designers] are competing with other disciplines, all of which want a piece of the technology pie. We have to move from competition to collaboration, to show...that a systems approach is the answer."[2] Systems designers echo this observation. Rettig observes, "to turn these ideas into effective solutions means acquiring good domain knowledge, representing it well, doing good instructional design, information design, human factors, and visual design."[3]

ED[4] accomplishes this goal. It uses a systems approach, but with a strong instructional design emphasis.

ED[4] Is a Process That Is Overdue

Design and development approaches with tools are needed in the field of EPSS design.

A documented process for creating EPSS is long overdue. Instructional experts recognize that EPSS designers need development methods and the tools to support development. Gery remarks, "There is little integrated information about or experience in designing and developing such integrated [EPSS] systems."[4] Gustafson, who is creating an EPSS to support instructional designers adds, "Our experience is that while some of our current knowledge and skill is applicable, a new or modified paradigm and many new tools are needed if we are to make the creation of EPSSs a technology rather than a craft."[5]

ED[4] provides tools for the design and development process as shown in Figure 6.2. These tools help EPSS designers work efficiently and productively. The job aid shown in Figure 6.2 is an interview sheet from the Define phase.

Table 7-1: Contextual Enquiry Observation Sheet	
Question Groups	**Typical Questions**
Tools used on the job	What tools do you use to support your job?
	How easy or difficult to use are the tools?
	Do you use electronic or paper-based tools?
	What tools do you need that you don't have?
	What tools do you use that are required?
	Do the required tools actually support job tasks?
	What percentage of time is spent using tools?
	What tools could the EPSS provide that you do not currently have?
Typical job tasks	What is a typical day like?
	What are typical job tasks?
	Are tasks necessary or distracting?
	What support exists for job tasks?
	What form of support exists? (experts, documentation)
	How long do tasks take to perform?
Hardware and software environment	What hardware do you use daily?
	What software do you use daily?
	What software do you need to perform job tasks?
Work environment	What person or organization do you depend on for job tasks?
	What are the disruptions to job tasks?
	How many disruptions are there to job tasks?
	What workarounds do you use for difficult job tasks?

Figure 6-2. Job Aid from the ED⁴ Process

ED⁴ Is a Process That Works

ED⁴ was used to create the LS Workbench EPSS.

ED⁴ is a process that Information Design & Consulting (IDC) at Digital Equipment Corporation uses to create cost-effective, instructional solutions. In 1993, IDC used the ED⁴ process to create an EPSS called the Learning Services (LS) Workbench. The Learning Ser-vices workbench resides on laptop computers and provides custom-ized proposal writing templates, information on the consulting process, and access to software demos for LS Consultants. LS Consultants use the Workbench to sell instructional solutions to customers. The workbench supports the entire consulting cycle from prospecting for clients through maintaining instructional solutions that customers purchase.

By using the ED⁴ process, EPSS designers created an EPSS that:

- Identified and met performer need (define phase).
- Was well planned and articulated (design phase).
- Is a high-quality software product (develop phase).
- Was easy to install and maintain (deliver phase).

ED⁴ Is Flexible and Creative

An approach that is flexible and allows for creative problem identification and solution is critical to good EPSS design. ED⁴ allows for creative problem solving.

The process is also very flexible. EPSS designers can tailor the process to the unique circumstances of their project. For example, performer needs assessment is a critical component of the Define phase of the ED⁴ process. A smaller EPSS project may choose to modify and do a small-scale needs assessment (small-group observation), while a larger, more complex project may perform a comprehensive assessment.

Process flexibility is also evident as the principles and activities within ED⁴ can apply to the design of any EPSS component – information database, learning modules, expert systems – as well as overall EPSS project management.

ED⁴ Is a Practical Approach

ED⁴ is a practical, hands-on approach.

Current literature on EPSS design points to the lack of solid, practical approaches to creating an EPSS. Designers need these tools for the full development cycle – from problem identification to post-delivery evaluation. ED⁴ is a practical approach that includes tools, tips, hints, and strategies for each phase of the design process (see Table 6-2). Throughout the book, the icon shown here designates a tool that EPSS developers can photocopy and use during the design and development process.

Table 6-2. ED⁴ Process: Design and Development Tools

Phase	Tools
Define	Context inquiry interview: observation sheet
	EPSS goal definition worksheet
	Guidelines for functional specification
	Project plan sections
	Creating an information architecture sheet
Design	Tools, templates and standards aid
	Considerations for EPSS user interface design

	Prototype review observation sheet
Develop	EPSS performance checklist
	Pre-implementation checklist
	Evaluation questions
Deliver	Project completion checklist

Overview of ED⁴ Process

The rest of this chapter previews the entire ED⁴ process and its phases. Chapters 7-10 describe each phase in detail.

Define: Transforming Performer Needs to an EPSS Plan

Define: focus on the performer and the foundation of the EPSS.

The Define phase is possibly the most important phase of the process. During this phase, the EPSS designers build the foundation for the entire project by concentrating on the performer.

ED⁴ provides specific tools to help EPSS designers observe, articulate, and relate to the performer and performer behavior. With this knowledge, the team can define EPSS goals and describe the technical functionality.

The phase also helps EPSS designers create a strategy for keeping the performer involved in the entire design and development process and for preparing the development team for supporting performers through the EPSS implementation. All of this information is available for design team, client, and performer use in these documents:

- Performer assessment
- Task assessment

- Software application requirements
- Project plan
- Project schedule
- Software functional specification
- Implementation strategy
- Support and maintenance plan

Design: Creating the Right Solution

Design: strategies, plans, tools, and templates

In the Define phase, the EPSS designer focuses on who the performer is, what the performer does and needs and on the software design that uniquely meets performer needs.

In the Design phase, the EPSS designer gathers content for the EPSS and creates the software authoring strategy that takes the plan from a paper ideal to a software reality.

ED[4] gives tools and templates that help the EPSS designer articulate the design into documents that the designer can share with the performer, the client, and the EPSS development team. They are visionary, yet practical, working documents that the team will use as a common ground of the articulated design.

These documents are:

- Information architecture
- Software authoring strategy
- Tools, templates and standards
- Detailed design specification
- User interface design

Develop: Creating a Quality Product

Develop: a team with a vision creates a software solution that meets performer needs.

In the Define and Design phases, the EPSS designer creates the foundation for a solid software design that matches the performer job needs.

In the Develop phase, the EPSS designer benefits from the work done in earlier phases. The team works together to create the software solution. The solution is in tune with performer needs and client requirements. ED[4] includes practical tools, strategies, hints, and tips to help the developers create an EPSS in the most cost-efficient manner possible. These aids translate to any EPSS regardless of size, cost, or complexity.

The software installation kit, whether on magnetic or optical media, is the outcome of the Develop phase.

Documents and software products in this phase are:

- Prototype
- Quality control approval
- Software installation kit
- Pre-implementation checklist

Deliver: Delivering the Solution

Deliver: a software product is delivered complete with a plan for the future.

Work done in the Define, Design, and Develop phases result in a robust, creative and cost-efficient EPSS that meets performer and client needs.

In the Deliver phase, the EPSS designers hand off the software solution to the client.

The EPSS designer works with the client to ensure a smooth transition from the development environment to the performer work environment. The designers work with the client and performers to evaluate the software to make sure it performs as it should. And the designer helps the client look to the future – in maintaining, supporting, and planning for enhancements to the EPSS.

On the developer side, the EPSS designers condense their experiences into a report of their experiences – tools they created, successes and failures – to assist other EPSS developers and improve the development process. Future EPSS teams benefit from the knowledge gained by current teams.

The experience and knowledge acquired are detailed in these documents:

- Software evaluation
- Follow-up plan
- Project file
- Post project review
- Project archival

Benefiting From the ED⁴ Process

There are many benefits of using the ED⁴ process. Besides a cost-efficient, and creative software solution that uniquely meets the performer needs, ED⁴ provides the tools that the development team needs throughout the process to be successful and the information the client needs to support and understand the process. describes the benefits to the client, the performer, and the EPSS design team.

Table 6-3. Benefits of ED[4]

ED[4] Phase		Benefits		
		Client	Performer	EPSS Team
Define	Input into EPSS design	✓	✓	✓
	Knowledge of performer needs	✓		✓
	Well-defined development plan	✓		✓
	Design that matches performer needs	✓	✓	✓
Design	Clearly defined authoring strategy			✓
	Solid EPSS design	✓	✓	✓
	Consistent EPSS interface	✓	✓	✓
	Consistent EPSS components	✓	✓	✓
	Software design tools			✓
Develop	Software development tools			✓
	Performer participation		✓	✓
	Robust software product	✓	✓	✓
	EPSS that matches performer needs	✓	✓	✓
Deliver	Delivery strategy	✓		✓
	Support for EPSS maintenance	✓	✓	
	Aids in planning EPSS upgrades	✓		

---

1 Fischer, Gerhard, Domain-Oriented Design; Paper presented at Proceedings of the Seventh Knowledge-Based Software Engineering Conference (IEEE), McLean, Va., September 20-23, 1992.

2 Wager, Walter W., "Instructional Systems Fundamentals: Pressures to Change", *Educational Technology*, February 1993.

3 Rettig, Marc, "Cooperative Software", *Communications of the ACM*, vol. 36, no. 4, April 1993.

4 Gery, Gloria J., "Training vs. Performance Support: Inadequate Training is Now Insufficient", *Performance Improvement Quarterly*, vol. 2, no. 3, 1989.

5 Gustafson, Ken L., "Instructional Design Fundamentals: Clouds on the Horizon", *Educational Technology*, February 1993.

ED⁴:

The Define Phase

THIS CHAPTER describes the Define phase, the first phase of the ED⁴ process for designing and developing Electronic Performance Support Systems.

Define Phase: Overview

Why "Define"?

Assess work performance and define EPSS technical functionality in the Define phase.

The Define phase is the most critical phase of the ED⁴ process. The key activity in this phase is the analysis of the performer and performance work environment. The definition of worker performance and the understanding of job tasks creates the philosophical and technical foundation of the EPSS. This defines the composition of the EPSS and how performers interact with it.

In addition, during the Define phase, the project manager begins building the EPSS team and establishing good client communications.

Why Define?

*Good planning is
the essence of the
Define phase.*

While a prospective homeowner would not let an architect begin building a home without a plan (the blueprint), sometimes clients want instructional designers and software engineers to begin creating a performance solution without devoting the time to planning and analysis. Often a client's reluctance to pay for the analysis is due to the urgency of the performance problem and the inability to see the value of the analysis.

ED[4] not only makes the design and development process "visible" (written documents of plans and analyses), but also *includes* clients and performers as active participants in shaping and defining the EPSS.

Table 7-1 describes the critical steps in the Define phase, who participates in the steps and the outcomes of the phase.

Table 7-1. Define Phase Steps

Step	Participants	Outcomes of Step
Assess performer needs	Instructional designer, performers, usability expert, client	Performance assessment
Define EPSS goals and requirements	Software engineer, instructional designer, performers, client	Software application requirements
Define EPSS technical functionality	Software engineer, instructional designer, client	Software functional specification
Plan the EPSS development process	Project manager, instructional designer, client	Project plan Project schedule

Assess Performer Needs

Knowing what
*performers do is
critical to good
EPSS design.*

Assessing performer needs is a suggested step in most instructional design and system design efforts. It is a *critical* step in EPSS design and development. An EPSS supports a person's job performance. Without thorough knowledge of the job, the EPSS team could spend a great deal of time and money creating an environment that does not match the work.

Performance assessments can involve different tactics and have different names depending on the instructional or system methodology used. In this chapter, the assessment for EPSS design includes the following tactics:

- Identify performers
- Observe performers at work
- Describe performer job tasks and processes
- Relate job tasks to EPSS roles

Identify Performers

Who is this mysterious group of people that we refer to as the "performers"? These are the people who are doing the work that the EPSS will support. It's important to identify a set of performers who will participate throughout the creation of the EPSS.

The people that the EPSS team selects should be at all levels of the job title, from novice to expert. Novices demonstrate the frustrations, roadblocks, and questions asked during the execution of a task. Experts demonstrate the best methods, tools, and techniques for performing the job. Performers who are in the range between novice and expert demonstrate some of both behaviors.

Find the Performers

The first place to find performers is through the client or sponsor. The performers' management is in the best position to describe employees' skill level and availability. Management also has a vested interest in making sure that the performers stay committed to the task of creating the EPSS.

If the sponsor or client isn't able to get the right people, Gause and Weinberg suggest using the broadcasting technique: "we post an announcement in the company newsletter, on bulletin boards, via electronic mail."[1] Through a simple interview or survey, the EPSS team can determine the skill level of the people who answer the call.

Identify Interrelated Performer Groups

The EPSS team identifies interdependencies between the performer group and other related work groups. It's possible that what a manager perceives as a performance problem might just be a redundant work process, or a bad "feed" from another group.

For example, a sales manager's report might be incorrect not because the manager is doing a poor job, but because the sales data the manager receives are incorrect. Or possibly the administrative assistant who enters the figures should be using a pie chart instead of a bar graph to display the figures.

Decide Level of Performer Involvement

It is very helpful to find a group of people who can assist the EPSS team from the early performer needs assessment to the final testing. If this is not possible, find out when performers are available and work around their schedule. All levels of skill ability might not be needed throughout the process.

For example, a master performer would be extremely helpful during the performance assessment, since the EPSS team needs to know the best methods for performing tasks. However, during prototyping, novice users would be better choices because the EPSS team would want to test how the EPSS affects task performance. Table 7-2 is a handy chart for noting performer level (expert, novice) and availability.

Track Performers Commitments

The instructional designer compiles a list of performers. These performers, given support of their management, can give important input into the initial design of the EPSS, as well as participate throughout all or specific phases of the software development effort.

Use the template in Table 7-2 to keep track of the performers and the dates or phases in which they will participate in the EPSS design and development.

Table 7-2. Performer List

Name	Performer Level	Phone	E-mail	Availability (√ or date)		
				Contextual Interview	Prototype Review	Pilot Test

Observe Performers at Work

Observe at work: see exactly what performers do on the job.

Contextual inquiry is "a means of gathering information from customers about their work practices and experiences. The contextual inquiry approach is based on field research techniques and focusing on interviewing users in their own context as they do actual work."[2]

Observing the performers in their own job context is extremely important for getting a real feel for job tasks, work patterns, and tools used.

Hints and strategies for performance observation.

Hints and Strategies

Holtzblatt and Beyer suggest the following for contextual inquiry interviews:[3]

- Conduct interviews with several performers at the same site on the same day to get a good view of the organization.

- Take two to three hours to interview each performer.

- Observe performers over a two-week time period.

- Observe performer during the interview, interrupting to get performers to articulate exactly what they are doing and why and how an EPSS could support their actions.

- Have instructional designers, usability experts, *and* software engineers perform the interviews. This keeps the EPSS design effort a "performer-centered" one.

- Analyze the information gathered from the interview and share it with the entire team.

- If possible, have a human factors expert facilitate the observation.

Table 7-3 is a checklist of the types of questions that instructional designers and software engineers ask as they observe the performers.

Table 7-3. Contextual Inquiry Interview: Observation Sheet

Question Groups	Typical Questions
Background	What is your job title?
	What are your primary job responsibilities?
	How many years of computer experience do you have? Using what systems?

Question Groups	Typical Questions
Tools used on the job	What tools do you use to support your job?
	How easy or difficult to use are the tools?
	Do you use electronic or paper-based tools?
	What tools do you need that you don't have?
	What tools do you use that are required?
	Do the required tools actually support job tasks?
	What percentage of time is spent using tools?
	What tools could the EPSS provide that you do not currently have?
Typical job tasks	What is a typical day like?
	What are typical job tasks?
	Are tasks necessary or distracting?
	What support exists for job tasks?
	What form of support exists? (experts, documentation)
	How long do tasks take to perform?
Hardware and software environment	What hardware do you use daily?
	What software do you use daily?
	What software do you need to perform job tasks?
Work environment	What person or organization do you depend on for job tasks?
	What are the disruptions to job tasks?
	How many disruptions are there to job tasks?
	What workarounds do you use for difficult job tasks?
Strategies for supporting job tasks	What electronic or paper-based tools would enhance job performance?
	What work or organization redesign strategies would help?

There are other strategies for defining work performance.

Note: Depending on the complexity of the EPSS, the designers may need to use additional strategies to define work performance. Strategies include interviews with managers, collecting and reviewing work-related documents or sending a survey to a large group of performers.

Describe Performer Job Tasks and Processes

Observing the performers provides a general picture of the performer and typical job tasks. In this next step, the instructional designer describes the tasks and works with the software engineer to determine the EPSS component that could support the job task.

List Performer Job Tasks

First, the instructional designer lists and groups the job tasks. The following is a template for the information to list about tasks. Group tasks are organized in meaningful ways based on EPSS team observ-ations, and show connections between tasks. Note: some designers prefer to place each task on a Post-It note or index card and to arrange notes on a blank wall to better show task interrelationships.

Regardless of the technique, the instructional designer lists the following information as shown in Table 7-4.

Table 7-4. Task Breakdown Sheet

Task	Work Required	Results	Tools Used	Support and Tools Needed

Decide Which Tasks to Support

From the performer observation will come an overwhelming list of tasks. The EPSS team must make decisions about what tasks to support. Not all tasks are critical to the job or are even part of the job. For example, in observing a bank teller, the EPSS team may realize that the teller creates a report that a customer service representative also creates. This is a "wasteful task." The teller is duplicating a coworker's work.

For this reason, the EPSS team should categorize and prioritize tasks according to type as shown in Table 7-5.

Table 7-5. Categorizing Tasks

Task Type	Explanation	Should the EPSS Support the Task?
Value adding	Adds value to the product	Yes
Ancillary	Critical to task that adds value	Yes
Distracting	Must be performed, but only adds value indirectly, so are distracting	Maybe
Wasteful	Does not add value or support task indirectly	No

Once the EPSS team categorizes the tasks, Carr suggests that the team do the following[4]:

- Discard wasteful tasks.

- Recommend that the client add distracting tasks to another job category. If this is not possible, automate these tasks within the EPSS.

- Decide if performers really need to perform ancillary tasks to support value-added tasks. If so, treat as a value-added task. If not, treat as a distracting task.

- Concentrate EPSS on value-added tasks.

Describe Job Process

Job tasks usually do not exist in isolation. Typically, the tasks are part of a job process or series of processes. Analyzing tasks also requires a look at these processes. According to Thomas, performers, "waste about one third of their time working inefficiently, but *delays* in their business processes waste 90 percent."[5]

The EPSS team looks critically at job processes. Organize tasks in a process flowchart. Decide if processes are efficient. If they are not, do not automate or add a bad process to the EPSS. While this may seem like a viable solution, it does a disservice to the client in the long run. Wiley says that the best solution is to, "help your customer is to begin by drawing a picture of their process using a structured flowchart, identifying measurement points, and then eliminating any steps that fail to add value." [6]

Use the question and solutions provided in looking at job processes as described in Table 7-6.

Table 7-6. Looking at Job Processes

Is the Process...?	If So, Then...
Redundant?	Decide which group performs the process, and advise management to plan for the transition of the process to the designated group.
Manual?	Consider automating the process within the EPSS.
Unnecessary?	Eliminate the process.
Confusing?	Flowchart the process to find areas of confusion. Work with management to clear up the process and re-flowchart the new, revised process.
Shared between groups?	Decide if process should be shared. If it should, make sure the EPSS supports all groups who perform the process.
Using dated methods and tools?	Research the current methods and tools and incorporate them into the EPSS.
At odds with company policy?	Research company policies and update the policy.
Not documented?	Flowchart or otherwise describe the process so that managers can approve any revisions.

Identify the Problems

From observing job tasks and processes and looking at ways to improve performance, the EPSS team has a good idea of what the performance problems and their solutions are. Performance problems can be the result of unclear expectations, inefficient processes, methods and tools, or poor links between related work groups.

Solutions can range from deleting a step in a process, adding a new tool or method, or redesigning a process or set of processes.

Use the chart in Table 7-7 to list performance problems and potential EPSS solutions.

Table 7-7: Performance Problems and Solutions

Performance Problems	EPSS Solutions

Relate Job Tasks to EPSS Roles

Choose EPSS components based on support performers need.

After describing job tasks, the instructional designer and software engineer begin to think in terms of *how* the EPSS could support these tasks. Carr (1992) defines four major roles that an EPSS might play.[7]

- **Librarian**
  Do performers need help finding information quickly and accurately?

- **Advisor**
  Do performers need guidance to perform tasks? Do they need to consult an expert?

- **Instructor**
  Do performers need on-demand instruction about specific parts of job tasks?

- **"Do"fer**
  Are there administrative tasks that are distracting to the performer? Could the EPSS perform these tasks?

Now the instructional designer and software engineer look at the list of job tasks in the context of these EPSS roles. The designers make some preliminary guesses of EPSS support and how the EPSS can assist in making job tasks easier or more efficient. This knowledge is included in the application requirements document (See Figure 7-1).

Relate EPSS Roles to EPSS Components

A subteam consisting of the instructional designer, software engineer, graphic designer, and usability expert work together. This subteam decides what the EPSS component strategy should be based on the performer needs and EPSS roles needed.

The strategy should match the roles that the performers needed "pre-EPSS." For example, suppose the team were designing for tax preparers who access the tax code, talk to experts about specific tax cases, and choose the correct forms based on customer input. The preparers' needs are:

- **Librarian**: Quick, easy, on-line access to the tax code
- **Advisor**: Guidance on how to choose the appropriate forms
- **Instructor**: Instruction on specific tax cases
- **"Do"fer**: Help in filling out forms (such as entering in the correct customer contact information)

The strategy given these needs would take into account the expertise of the EPSS team, the technology, budget, and timelines.

For example, the solution for the tax preparers given a PC, client/server environment with hypermedia might be that shown in Table 7-8.

Table 7-8. Performer Needs, EPSS Roles and EPSS Strategy

Performer Need	EPSS Role Needed	EPSS Strategy
Quick, easy, on-line access to the tax code	Librarian	Hypertext knowledge base
Guidance on how to choose the appropriate forms	Advisor	Coach (expert system)
Instruction on specific tax cases	Instructor	Hypertext instruction
Help in filling out forms	"Do"fer	• Customized templates for Microsoft Word • Access to knowledge base for customer information

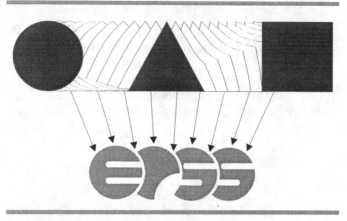

Figure 7-1. Performance Assessment Informs the EPSS

Define EPSS Goals and Requirements

Based on the performance observations, the EPSS team knows the performance tasks and processes and is ready to identify the high-level goals of the EPSS.

Do not concentrate solely on what the actual EPSS components will be – instead the instructional designer and software engineer should think in terms of how the EPSS could improve, support, and streamline job tasks. It may help to use the worksheet in Table 7-9.

Table 7-9. EPSS Goal Definition Worksheet

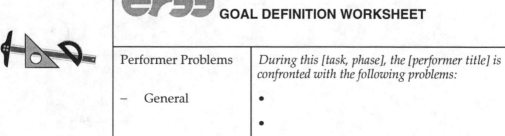 **GOAL DEFINITION WORKSHEET**	
Performer Problems	*During this [task, phase], the [performer title] is confronted with the following problems:*
– General	• •
– Task related	• •

EPSS GOAL DEFINITION WORKSHEET	
EPSS Requirements:	*The EPSS should enable the [performer title] to:*
– Business	•
	•
– Organizational	•
	•
– End user	•
	•
– Technology	•
	•
EPSS Limitations	*The following limitations exist:*
– Technical	•
	•
– Organizational	•
	•
– Time	•
	•
– Resource	•
	•

Categorize Requirements

The list of what the performers need might be long. Budget and time constraints may prevent the EPSS team from implementing everything that the performers need.

If this is the case, categorize the requirements. Certain requirements may be critical to performance improvement and should be implemented immediately. Other requirements may be implemented in a later release of the software. Still other requirements may be impossible to implement or in conflict with other more important requirements.

Gause and Weinberg recommend that designers use the following codes to categorize requirements:[8]

- P – Possibility, to be achieved now
- D – Deferred, to be achieved in a later version
- A – Absolute impossibility, to be dropped from consideration

Decide Non-Goals

If the EPSS team categorizes certain requirements as unachievable, they should be listed as non-goals on the application requirements documents. This sets the expectation with the performers and clients that the EPSS has some limits.

Create a Requirements Document

Create a written document outlining work performance and general EPSS goals.

At this point in the Define phase, the EPSS team has a complete picture of the performer's job and job tasks, and high level goals.

The software engineer compiles this information in a *software application requirements* document. This document includes:

- Performer job tasks and process
- Performer problems and solutions
- Performer list
- EPSS roles
- EPSS goals and requirements

Note that these are *high-level* goals (see Table 7-10 for examples). Specific technical goals include the best work of the entire EPSS team as they create the software functional specification. Both documents should be flexible and iterative, as changes in the performers' job, the client's expectations, the technology involved, and the skills of the EPSS team can affect the EPSS goals. Table 7-10 gives examples of some of the goals of the Learning Services Workbench EPSS.

Table 7-10. Goals: Learning Services Workbench EPSS

Goals for the "Preparing Account" Phase of the Selling Cycle	
Problems:	
Preparing	During this phase of the account, the Learning Services (LS) consultant is confronted with the following problems:
	• Difficulty locating products and services information
	• Difficulty locating resource information

Requirements:

Preparing   The EPSS should enable the LS Consultant to:

- Locally access resource information directly through the LS EPSS library

- Remotely connect through the terminal emulator to access resource information.

Review the Requirements Document

The designers meet with the client and performers for review and sign-off. Following the review, the designers pass the document on to the EPSS team. The team uses the document as a basis for the technical functionality of the EPSS. The software engineer and technical team define specific technical functionality in a *functional specification* document (see Figure 7-2).

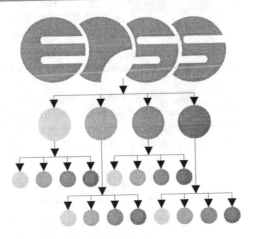

Figure 7-2. Transition to Detailed Design

Define EPSS Technical Functionality

The *software functional specification* describes the high-level, technical functionality of the EPSS. In this document, the EPSS team translates the knowledge gained during the up-front analysis into the technical framework of the EPSS. The software engineer creates this document with input from a usability or user interface expert, project manager and instructional designer.

The software engineer creates a high-level system functionality specification.

This is a flexible document that may change as the system develops, but is a beginning point for the EPSS team, a reference point for the client, and a verification that the system meets performer needs.

Functional Specification Guidelines

While the format of the software functional specification depends on the software authoring environment (coding-oriented versus object-oriented), Table 7-11 describes the general sections the document contains and suggestions for the type of information each section could include. Seeing complete examples of a functional specification would be useful, but is beyond the scope of this book.

Table 7-11. Guidelines for Functional Specification

Sections	Information to Include
System overview	General description of EPSS including overall system goals and definitions of system entities such as expert systems, hypertext, and so on. This section could include system flowcharts to further illustrate connections between EPSS components.
System detail	Descriptions of EPSS components in greater detail including file names and structures, and component interactions and connections. Flowcharts, tables, and graphics are useful to show the connections between different EPSS components.
Environment	Hardware and software environment for EPSS installation, including system capability, speed, monitor/display capabilities, color resolution

Sections	Information to Include
Quality specifications	Definition of quality goals for the EPSS such as ease of use, reliability, and maintainability, including how EPSS meets those goals.
General system specifications	Global specifications such as the system storage capacity, performance, installation, internationalization specifications, and so on.
Training	User documentation and training needed to accompany the EPSS installation.
System limitations	Hardware or software limitations such as inability to mobile compute.
User interface	Samples (graphics or sketches) of user interface design.
Support and maintenance	Describes how the EPSS team will support the EPSS once it's installed and describes future releases of the software.

Review the Functional Specification

Like the requirements document, the EPSS team meets with the client and the performers to make sure that the functional specification matches their expectations. A useful strategy is a walkthrough of the specification – the software engineer goes through the specification section by section. The engineer explains each section and answers any questions.

Once the functional specification is in place, the project manager plans the development process.

Plan the EPSS Development Project

Imagine an EPSS team that is excited and ready to go. They have created an exceptional design that the client has approved. The team is eager to start the work. But before they do, the project manager must create a plan.

EPSS development is an intricate and interrelated process. Software engineers depend on the graphic designer and usability expert to create the "look and feel" of the user interface. Instructional designers depend on the software engineers to create the software that drives a tutorial. The software engineer who creates an expert system must depend on a coworker who is creating the user interface.

Without careful coordination, the development process can become confused and convoluted. It is at this point that the project manager begins his or her critical role in:

- Planning the development process
- Planning for support and maintenance

Plan the Development Process

Create a project plan: a contract for schedule and budget between you and the client.

Once the application requirements document and functional specification exist, the project manager plans the design and development process. Planning tools vary from company to company, but the following research should be done and information gathered and collected into a *project plan*.

The project manager writes the project plan and includes the information that follows. The client reviews and signs off on this plan that serves as the formal contract between the client and the EPSS team.

Guidelines for Project Plan

The format of the project plan varies. Most project plans include the general sections described in Table 7-12. Most of these sections are straightforward and are a compilation of information the EPSS team has been gathering during the Define phase.

Creating the project and budget is somewhat more complicated. Specific information on these topics follows Table 7-12.

Table 7-12. Project Plan Sections

Project Plan Section	Description
PROJECT DESCRIPTION	
Overview	Describes what the name of the process is, why the EPSS is being developed, and the need that the EPSS fills.
Audience description	Describes the performer group including their characteristics, needs, job classifications and experience levels.
Goals	Explains the goals of the EPSS as described in the *application requirements document*.
Non-goals	Explains goals that either are beyond the scope of this project or are planned for future releases of the software as described in the *application requirements document*.

DESIGN AND DEVELOPMENT STRATEGIES

Performance improvement strategy

Explains the strategies that will be used to meet performer needs. This section includes why certain EPSS components were chosen and the expected performance outcomes.

Technology strategy

Describes the authoring hardware and software languages or environments that the team will use to create the EPSS.

- Specify software version numbers and hardware model numbers.

- Include any developer tools that will be used to optimize the development process.

Testing strategy

Describe any performer testing that will take place including:

- Prototyping

- Acceptance testing

- Final system testing

Quality control strategy

Describes all steps taken by the EPSS team to ensure a quality EPSS including:

- Performer and client reviews

- Technical reviews

- Inter-team reviews

- Copy editing

- Software debugging, testing and validation

- Design and development tools and templates and writing, screen design, and programming standards

RESOURCE REQUIREMENTS

Development resources

Describes the exact number of resources required by job title and level of involvement in the project (Ex. full-time, part-time, 20 hours per fiscal quarter, and so on.)

Implementation resources	Describes the type of system that the EPSS will run on and the resources needed to install, support, and maintain the system.
DELIVERABLES	
	Describe the exact deliverables including:
	• Type, format and number of software kits (Ex. "15 3 x 5" Macintosh-formatted DSDD diskettes)
	• Number and format of documentation that will accompany the EPSS
	• Software specialist support included for support and maintenance
PROJECT MANAGEMENT	
Schedule	See Page 7-20.
Risks and dependencies	Describes contingencies, events or situations beyond the control of the EPSS team that would affect the project schedule, budget or deliverables such as:
	• Hardware/software availability
	• Change in project scope (due to client or performer requests)
	• Engineering slips (if EPSS depends on an external software product)
Budget	See following text section

Create the Project Schedule and Budget

Create a high-level project schedule with major milestones such as completion of functional specification, prototype, pilot test, and project completion date. The project manager creates the more detailed schedules after completing the functional specification. At that time, the project manager has a clearer idea of system components and software design time required per component. Table 7-13 is a portion of the schedule from the Learning Services Workbench EPSS project.

Item Description	Authoring	System Integration and Testing
Tools and templates	July 2	August 1
Information sheets	June 22	August 1
Customer presentations	July 31	August 1
EPSS tools	June 25	
• Navigator		Nov. 1
• Grabit		Nov. 1
MS applications	June 25	
• MS Word		"
• PowerPoint		"
• Excel		"
Software demos	Sept. 30	Nov. 1

Table 7-13. Sample Project Schedule: LS Workbench Project

The client may preset the project budget, or the EPSS team creates a budget based on the complexity of the software development effort.

Chapter 8 of this book, ED⁴: *The Design Phase*, describes these steps in greater detail.

Plan for Support and Maintenance

It's never too early to plan for the future. Even though development of the EPSS has not begun, the project manager must prepare for when the EPSS will be installed and maintained on the client's system. The project manager must plan now for:

- Supporting the client group during EPSS implementation
- Maintaining the EPSS after implementation

Plan for Implementation Support

The project manager meets with the client now to determine the type of support that they will need during implementation. The following are types of support to suggest and recommendations for how to plan for the support.

- **Software Release Strategy**
  Decide now how the EPSS software will be released. Will it be implemented in one or several releases? How will the software be installed and implemented? How will the EPSS team respond to change requests? With patch kits or new kits?

- **Hotline**
  This is either a phone line or on-line repository for customer questions during installation. The hotline may also be used to collect performer feedback, software errors, or requests for additional EPSS functionality.

  Plan for: Person to answer the phone line or on-line repository; person to create the on-line repository; phone lines.

- **Training**
  The customer may need a user guide, installation guide, and training session to accompany the software. These materials help performers get started using the EPSS.

  Plan for: Instructional designer or writer to write guides or develop training; costs for printing and binding guides; instructor to teach training session; cost for participants to attend the session.

- **On-site Support**
  The customer may require a software specialist to install the EPSS and provide support for the performers in the early stages of use.

  Plan for: Software specialist's time for one to two days.

Plan for Post-Implementation Maintenance

There are steps that the EPSS team can take now to make maintenance an easier task. Maintenance refers to correcting, inserting, extending, and enhancing the baseline (first version) EPSS.

The following are ways to plan for maintenance:

- **Organize Performer Requests**
  While assessing performer needs, gathering performer requirements and defining technical functionality, create a mechanism for documenting any requests that cannot be implemented in this release of the EPSS. The mechanism can be as simple as an on-line file or as complex as an on-line bulletin board. Assign time for a software engineer to organize these requests and decide if additional releases of the EPSS are needed. If so, line up the resources and budget now to work on future software releases.

- **Emphasize Documentation**
  One of the major obstacles for software maintainers is incomplete, dated documentation. Critical documentation for maintainers include project plans, functionality requests, functional specifications, and design documents. Encourage the EPSS team to keep these and other relevant documents up-to-date and in an on-line project directory or folder.

- **Anticipate the Future**
  Anticipate the future. Keep track of the technology that is used to create the EPSS. Anticipate requests from the performer group, and keep in contact so that the EPSS team can respond to any changes in their work environment. Plan for implementing change based on this knowledge.

- **Allocate Resources and Budget for Maintenance**
  Based on future needs, submit a budget for future releases of the EPSS and allocate resources for these efforts.

Project-manage the Define Phase

The project manager is establishing some critical work patterns during the Define phase. They are:

Manage

- **Set client expectations**
  The client has given input into the EPSS design through conversations and reviews of the project plan, application requirements document, and functional specification. Maintain this level of involvement to ensure that the EPSS meets client expectations.

- **Establish good client and project team communications**
  Define a communications strategy with the client. This strategy ensures that the project manager informs the client in the format that the client requires or prefers.

Document

- **Project file**
  Start a *project file.* This on-line or paper-based repository contains all project-related documents to establish continuity during the project and serves as a historical record for future projects. The project file includes the following:

    - Project contact list: Names, phone numbers and E-mail addresses of all team members including the client and performers
    - Project status reports
    - Project schedules
    - Budget spreadsheets (original and any addenda)
    - Memos documenting any decisions
    - Project proposals and plans
    - Addenda to plan documenting changes in budget or schedule
    - Software design documents
    - Performer observations
    - Project requirements documents
    - Prototyping information
    - Acceptance test results
    - Approval or sign-off sheets
    - Quality control checklist
    - Change control documentation
    - Post project reviews

- **Project plan**
  Make sure that a signed project plan is in the project file. This document serves as a contract between the development group and the client.

- **Quality guidelines**
  The project plan begins the process of building quality into the EPSS development process. The plan includes quality steps such as technical reviews, performer involvement, and prototyping. Each phase in ED[4] adds to this quality process. Each EPSS team member should be aware of and follow this process.

Overcoming Obstacles

Table 7-14 describes some of the obstacles that EPSS designers face during the Define phase, and strategies for overcoming these obstacles.

Table 7-14. Common Design Phase Obstacles and Solutions

Obstacle	Solutions
Getting organizational support	Show return on investment (see Chapter 3; *Justifying EPSS*, for strategies).
	Keep client and performers closely involved in the process.
	Demonstrate the power of EPSS through presentations to upper management.
Correctly assessing needs	Identify performers who are at performer different skill levels.
	Look for non-verbal as well as verbal cues regarding performance problems.
	Work with management to gather information relative to the performer's job.
	Identify all inter-relationships between the performer and other groups and assess the impact of these inter-relationships.
	Document all interviews and observations.
	Review your observations and conclusions with performers.
Creating the right EPSS strategy	Correctly and fully assess performer needs.
	Understand the limitations of the technology.
	Map performer needs to potential EPSS responses.
	Provide several EPSS responses to specific performer needs to meet different learning styles.

---

1 Gause Donald C., and Weinberg, Gerald M., *Exploring Requirements: Quality Before Design*, New York: Dorset House, 1989.

2 Holtzblatt, Karen and Jones, Sandra, *Contextual Inquiry: Principles and Practices*, Digital Technical Report DEC-TR 729, Digital Equipment Corporation, 1990.

3 Hotlzblatt, K. and Beyer, H. "Making Custiomer-Centred Design Work for Teams, " *Communications of the ACM*, vol. 36, no 10, October 1993.

4 Carr, Clay, "Performance Support Systems – the Next Step?," CBT Directions, June 1992.

5 Quoted in Arthur, Lowell Jay, *Improving Software Quality: An Insider's Guide to TQM*, New York: Wiley, 1993.

6 Quoted in Arthur, Lowell Jay, *Improving Software Quality: An Insider's Guide to TQM*, New York: Wiley, 1993.

7 Carr, Clay, "PSS! Help When You Need It," *Training & Development*, June 1992.

8 Gause, Donald C., and Weinberg, Gerald M., *Exploring Requirements: Quality Before Design*, New York: Dorset House, 1989.

ED^4:

The Design Phase

THIS CHAPTER describes the Design phase, the second phase of the ED^4 process for designing and developing Electronic Performance Support Systems.

Design Phase: Overview

What Is "Design"?

The EPSS team creates and tests the detailed design in the Design phase.

In the Design phase, the EPSS team creates a flowchart or storyboards of the detailed design (see Figure 8-1). This working document is the blueprint that the software engineers and instructional designers use to create the EPSS. The EPSS team tests the design with the performers using either rapid prototyping, flowchart or storyboard reviews, or a combination of these methods.

The EPSS team also identifies and creates the development tools, templates, and standards that will help make a quality software product.

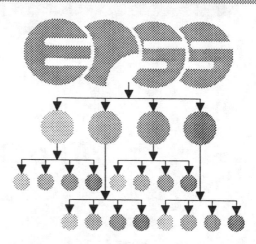

Figure 8-1. Creating the EPSS Detailed Design

Why Design?

Documenting the design prevents misconceptions between the EPSS team, client, and performers.

Children in the United States play a game called "whisper down the lane." Sitting in a circle, the "leader" whispers a message into the ear of the nearest child, that child whispers the message in the ear of the next child. The message passes around the circle until it returns to the leader, who repeats it aloud for the group. Often, the message is nothing like the original.

This distortion of an original concept can happen in an EPSS development effort. A client relays ideas about a software product to a project manager, who passes them to a lead software engineer, who passes them to one or more software engineers. If these ideas pass by this many people *verbally*, with each person adding individual perceptions and biases, the final product may vary greatly from the original concept.

The ED[4] process helps prevent these misconceptions by giving developers the tools to articulate the EPSS design *in verbal and written form.* This provides a feedback loop between the EPSS team, the client, and the performers. ED[4] also gives strategies for ensuring consistency throughout the Design and Develop phases.

Table 8-1 describes the Design phase steps, including participants in and outcomes of each step.

Table 8-1. Design Phase Steps

Step	Participants	Outcomes
Design the EPSS	Software engineer, instructional designer, usability expert, graphic designer, performer	Content design strategy, standards and tools, detailed design
Test the EPSS design	Software engineer, instructional designer, usability expert, performer	Tested design

Design the EPSS

Creating the EPSS design is an iterative process that varies from project to project. Design methods depend on the EPSS type and complexity and EPSS team preferences. Regardless of approach and method, the EPSS team should follow these steps:

- Identify, collect, and design information (if applicable)
- Create tools, templates, and standards
- Structure the EPSSdesign

Identify, Collect and Design Information

This step applies for EPSSs that have knowledge bases, instruction, help, or expert systems. In systems with these components, there is information – reference material, facts and figures, and expert advice – that the instructional designer must identify, collect and design.

Identify and Collect Information

Work with performers to gather original information. This information may be documents such as manuals, technical reference materials, forms, information sheets, pricing information, and so on.

Information may be in verbal form. The instructional designer gathers this information by interviewing the performers and observing work behaviors (see Chapter 7; *The Define Phase* for interviewing and observation techniques).

Verify with performers and management that the information is current, complete, and accurate.

Design Information

Develop an information architecture strategy.[1] Decide how information flows through the EPSS as shown in Table 8-2. The EPSS team decides:

- How to *structure* the information
- How performers will *access* the information
- The *context* within which performers access information

Table 8-2. Creating an Information Architecture

Categories	Strategies	Questions to Ask
Structure	Hierarchical	Is information arranged hierarchically (top down)?
	Associative	Is the information arranged non-sequentially, so that performers can browse through as needed?
Access	Browse sequences	Do performers move vertically or horizontally through an information topic?
		Do performers move horizontally or vertically from topic to topic?
	Jumps	Do performers have one-step access to related topics (*a jump*)?
		How many jumps does the system allow?
		How does the system help the performers maintain context (where they are and where they have been)?
	Pop-ups	Does the system provide further explanation of terms and concepts within a topic (*a pop-up*)?
		Are pop-ups in graphic, text, video or audio form or a combination of these methods?

Categories	Strategies	Questions to Ask
Context	History	Do performers have a visual representation of the topics they have viewed?
		Does the system allow performers to move quickly to previously viewed topics?
	Maps	Do performers have a visual representation of where they are within an information set?

Organize the information into small, stand-alone units. Each unit of information should be independent – performers who are using the EPSS should not have to read earlier information to understand current information. Many instructional designers use Horn's Information Mapping methodology to ensure that information units are discrete and independent. [2]

Format Information

Use hypertext authoring guidelines to format information. Rely less on text and more on tables, graphics, and lists to relay information and use a definite strategy to link information.

Share Information

Decide how information will flow through the EPSS. Will information be available in any EPSS component (including in customized software applications)? How will performers be able to use information – will they be able to print it, edit it? Will performers be able to print and use graphics? Are there technical issues in giving performers the information access they require?

The instructional designer and software engineer may use flowcharting or storyboarding techniques to show interrelationships.

Create Tools, Templates, and Standards

Tools, standards, and templates help keep the EPSS team consistent, efficient, and productive.

Creating tools, templates, and standards is a critical step in the Design phase. Use of these helps the EPSS team work consistently, efficiently, and productively.

- **Tools**
  Software or paper-based aids for any EPSS team member that the project manager purchases or that the EPSS team creates.

For example, instructional designers may purchase software that automates the performance needs analysis process or create a macro that replaces a symbol in a help file with the appropriate software coding.

- **Templates**
  Software or paper guides that format information or specifications that EPSS team members use repeatedly.

  For example, graphic designers may create a file that includes the exact proportions, font sizes, colors, and other formatting for a specific group of graphics.

- **Standards**
  Instructions, information, styles, or formatting that EPSS team members must follow.

  For example, software engineers may create software coding standards for writing and documenting their software code that makes all coding consistent and easy for new EPSS team members to read, use, and edit.

The instructional designer and software engineer develop the tools, templates and standards (Table 8-3) for the writing and programming teams.

Table 8-3. Determining Tools, Templates, and Standards

	For Software Engineers	For Instructional Designers
Tools	Software authoring Software coding Flowcharting	Hypertext authoring Computer-based training (CBT) authoring Graphics
Templates	Screen layout Hypertext	Screen layout CBT screen layout Graphics

	For Software Engineers	For Instructional Designers
Standards	Coding Annotating software code Flowcharting Filenaming	Writing Graphics CBT storyboarding Filenaming Key wording Indexing

Structure the EPSS Design

With an information design strategy, tools, templates, and standards in place, the software engineers finalizes the design. The work completed in this step make up the *detailed design*.

In writing and describing the design, the software engineer should use technical language for the EPSS team and nontechnical language for client and performer reviews.

The software engineer:

- Finalizes and flowcharts the EPSS component strategy
- Designs the user interface

Finalize and Flowchart the EPSS Component Strategy

In the Define phase, the instructional designer and software engineer identified the EPSS support roles (librarian, advisor, instructor, and "do"fer). The EPSS team leaders then translated these support roles into a conceptual view of potential EPSS components (in the software functional specification).

In the Design phase, the software engineer moves from a conceptual view to a concrete view. The software engineer chooses specific EPSS components based on programmer ability, technology, and budget. The EPSS team puts final touches on the interrelationships between components.

At this time, the software engineer writes the detailed software development schedule based on the final system design. See Table 8-4 for a sample schedule.

Table 8-4. Portion of Schedule from LS Workbench Project

Item Description	Authoring				Integration
	Design and Development	MS-Word Formatting	Hypertext Coding	Keyword Coding	
Tools and templates	Complete	June 12	June 18	July 2	August 1
Information sheets	"	June 15	June 21	June 22	August 1
Customer presentations	July 1	July 8	July 18	July 31	August 1
EPSS tools					
Navigator	June 5	June 12	June 18	June 25	Nov 1
Grabit	"	"	"	"	"
MS applications	Complete				
MS Word	"	"	"	"	
Software demos	Aug. 30	Sept. 12	Sept. 20	Sept. 30	Sept. 30
PowerPoint	"	"	"	"	"
Excel	"	"	"	"	"

Design the User Interface

An easy-to-use, intuitive user interface is critical to the performer's perception of the EPSS.

The user interface is the performer's "view" into the EPSS, and it is the way in which the performer interacts with the software. As a subteam, the software engineer, instructional designer, and human factors expert create the interface.

- Designing a common, easy-to-use, intuitive, and industry standard user interface is critical to how the performer perceives the EPSS. Raybould quotes Bonstra regarding the benefits of a common user interface:[3]

- Users can run more software (two and one half times more).

- It offers the user a 25 percent productivity improvement.

- Training time for learning new applications is reduced by 25 percent.

User Interface Design Approaches

Three user interface design approaches.

Raybould recommends three design approaches for creating the user interface. Approach one is the most desirable of the three.[4]

1. Use one primary development platform that gives you control over the user interface, and use add-on tools or routines that provide base functions that can be integrated within the primary interface.

2. Choose development platforms which all conform to a widely available user interface standard, such as *Windows* and *Presentation Manager* for IBM compatible PCs, *MultiFinder* for Macintosh computers, or *X-Windows* for UNIX workstations.

3. Use one primary development platform and integrate other tools by using external program calls or by integrating them all at the source code level.

Testing the interface design *before* the EPSS team finalizes it is critical to creating an EPSS user interface that really supports performer tasks.

User Interface Design Principles

Schneiderman describes the "eight golden rules of dialog design":[5]

- Strive for consistency
- Enable frequent users to use shortcuts
- Offer informative feedback
- Design dialogs to yield closure
- Offer simple error handling
- Permit easy reversal of actions
- Support internal locus of control
- Reduce short-term memory load

The following list includes questions the EPSS team should ask as they design the interface.

Questions

- How much interactivity is available to performers?

- Are all screen elements clearly marked?

- Is the screen clean and uncluttered?

- Are color, shading, and graphics used effectively?

- Will there be a visual representation of the path the performer takes through the EPSS?

- How easy is it to navigate through the EPSS?

- Is there a simple way to return to the main screen?

Note: This is only a sample of the questions that the EPSS team should ask. The team should expand this list based on the unique EPSS needs.

Test the EPSS Design

Testing in the Design phase involves reviews and walkthroughs of the detailed design with performers and within the EPSS team.

Perform Project Team Reviews

Review the EPSS design with EPSS team members, the client, and performers.

Design is an iterative and collective effort, with constant communication between the software developers. Design reviews and walkthroughs keep the design consistent and ensure that the development does not stray away from the original intent of the client and the performers.

Spitzer urges developers to use an iterative development approach, "Using the iterative approach during the design phase involves getting as much feedback as possible, as early as possible...Too often, iteration is viewed as a sign of weakness or indecision, but nothing could be further from the truth...Continual improvement is one of the most critical features of successful intervention design."[6]

Coordinate Performer Reviews

Design reviews with performers is critical at this point. In the Define phase, the EPSS team developed a list of performers to participate during the design and development process.

The project manager contacts the reviewers and schedules time for them to review the design to make sure the EPSS team's interpretation still matches the performer's environment.

While walkthroughs of the design are difficult at this time, the EPSS team helps the performers envision the future system through storyboards or flowcharts. If there are PC tools that support it, the EPSS team creates a small prototype of a representative section of the system and get performer reaction to it.

The EPSS team must be willing to revise the design based on this input.

Project-manage the Design Phase

The project management activities for this phase revolve around building the EPSS team and keeping the client and performer involved in the design process.

Manage

- **Set client expectations**
  Include the client in all design decisions, from informing the client of performer reactions to the detailed design (and consequent changes to the design), to having the client sign off on the detail design document.

- **Continue to build the EPSS team**
  Continually assess the EPSS team's interaction and productivity. Make sure the EPSS team is working well together, and that all members are living up to their individual and collective responsibilities. Regularly scheduled EPSS team meetings are important for keeping communication open.

Document

- **Track the project budget**
  Keep abreast of how much money has been spent based on the original budget. Is the budget on track? Have there been unforeseen expenses? Negotiate with the client if the development effort is over or under budget.

- **Update the project file**
  Continue to make the project file a priority. Add the detailed design document to the file, along with any important memos or authorizations.

Overcoming Obstacles

Table 8-5 describes common obstacles in the Design phase, and strategies for overcoming these obstacles.

Table 8-5. Common Design Phase Obstacles and Solutions

Obstacles	Solutions
Creating the best design	Involve performers and clients in the design process.
	Use object-oriented analysis and design software.
	Create a visual representation of the design (flowcharts, storyboards, or prototype) for programmer and performer review.
	Use PC technology to its fullest capability.
Articulating the design in lay terms for performers	Remember that performers are not programmers – describe the design in simple terms.
	Remember to incorporate the performer's work language (acronyms, lingo, and slang) into the design.
Prioritizing and incorporating review comments	Schedule time for review and changes to the design (if necessary).
	Rate and prioritize review comments, incorporating the highest-rated comments.
	File low-priority review comments for future EPSS enhancements.

1 Microsoft Corporation. Windows Help Authoring Guide, (Available on Internet), Redwood, MA, 1993.

2 Horn, Robert E. Strategies for Developing High-Performance Documentation. Waltham, Mass.: Information Mapping, Inc., 1990.

3 Raybould, Barry. "A Modular Approach to Electronic Performance Support," Data Training, March-April 1992.

4 Raybould, Barry. "A Modular Approach to Electronic Performance Support," Data Training, 1992.

5 Schneiderman, Ben. Designing the User Interface: Strategies for Effective Human-Computer Interaction. Reading, Mass.: Addison-Wesley, 1992.

6 Spitzer, Dean R. "The Design and Development of Effective Interventions," In Handbook of Performance Technology: A Comprehensive Guide for Analyzing and Solving Performance Problems in Organizations,.eds Harold D. Stolovitch and Erica D. Keeps, San Francisco: Jossey-Bass, 1992.

ED⁴:

The Develop Phase

THIS CHAPTER describes the Develop phase, the third phase of the ED⁴ process for developing Electronic Performance Support Systems.

Develop Phase: Overview

Create the EPSS components in the develop phase.

In the Define and Design phases of the ED⁴ process, the team creates a strong foundation for the EPSS. The team puts a detailed design, standards, templates, and tools in place to assist the EPSS developers.

In the Develop phase, the team creates the EPSS components. If the team spent enough time creating a specific, detailed design, the development effort is relatively painless. Spitzer remarks, "The extent and difficulty of development will depend largely on how clearly the design has been specified and on the types of materials to be developed. The effort required for development is often inversely proportional to the effort invested in design."[1] Table 9-1 describes the Develop phase steps, including participants and outcomes of each step.

Table 9-1. Develop Phase Steps

Step	Participants	Outcome of Step
Create a prototype	Software engineer, instructional designer	Working prototype
Plan the development effort	Usability expert, graphic designer, performer	
Develop EPSS components	EPSS development team	Working system
Test and revise the EPSS		Pilot test results
Build software installation kit	Software engineer, instructional designer	Software kit Installation procedures
Prepare to implement the EPSS	Project manager, client, sponsor, EPSS development team	Pre-implementation checklist

Create a Prototype

A prototype is a preliminary version of the EPSS, user interface, or representative components.

A *prototype* is a preliminary version of either the overall system, the user interface, or one or several representative components (see Figure 9-1). With PC authoring tools, the team can develop the prototype quickly and early in the development process.

Creating a prototype makes good business sense since EPSS development involves a major commitment of funding, resources, and time. Spitzer says of any performance intervention, "If the stakes are high, or if there will be a major production effort involved, it is usually advisable to produce and test a prototype version of the intervention materials before final production and implementation."[2]

The team should follow a scaled-down version of the team's actual development process and the recommendations described in later sections of this chapter to create the prototype.

Figure 9-1. Different Types of Prototypes

Testing the Prototype

Have performers test the prototype using a representative work task.

Once the prototype exists, the project manager should contact a representative number of performers to review it. It is extremely useful for the software engineers to follow this procedure during the test:

1. Give performers a sample job task to perform using the prototype:
    -   Choose a task from the performer needs assessment that the team performed in the Define phase.

    -   Break the task down into small, observable behaviors and actions.

2. Observe performers and ask questions as they perform the task (see Figure 9-2 for an observation sheet template that the team can use to critique the prototype).

3. Compile information from all performer reviews.

4. Decide if the prototype is effective. If it is, continue development. If is it not, prioritize feedback and revise detailed design.

    The observer should closely watch the performer's behaviors. Critical questions to ask while observing include the following. Are there moments when the performer is frustrated or puzzled? Are there long pauses (indicating that the performer is unsure of what to do next)? Does the performer ask questions that cannot be answered by the EPSS?

Prototype Review: Observation Sheet	
Prototype Description:	
Performer Name:	Job Title:
Task Description:	
Projected Task Time:	Actual Task Time:
Task Observations:	Questions to Ask: • What were you thinking when you got to this point? • What was it you needed here? • Did you have a question here? • What was your reaction to that? • Is there anything you needed here that you didn't have?
Observed by:	Date and time:
• Recommendations Based on Observations:	

Figure 9-2. Prototype Review Observation Sheet

Revising the Prototype

The prototype becomes the template for the EPSS development effort.

The software engineer and instructional designer should prioritize the recommendations from the review and decide which they can implement. Recommendations that are worthwhile, but that the team cannot implement because of budget, time, or technological restrictions can go into the project file as future enhancements to the EPSS.

The prototype becomes the basis or even the template for the rest of the software development effort.

Plan the Development Effort

The project manager decides the work strategy, work tasks, assignments and prepares the team for EPSS development.

The project manager is critical to the success of the development effort. The project manager should know the strengths and weaknesses of the team and makes project assignments based on this knowledge.

The project manager should work to create a team environment, where team members share information, shortcuts, and critiques.

Prior to the actual development effort, the project manager should:

- Decide the work strategy
- Determine work tasks
- Schedule and assign the work
- Prepare the team for development

Decide Work Strategy

The work strategy is the ways in which team members will work toward common goals. Work strategy issues to resolve include:

- Explain how to share information
- Create communication vehicles
- Decide team and individual work strategies
- Identify strategies for problem resolution
- Decide parallel and sequential tasks
- Coordinate work hand-offs

Explain How to Share Information

Provide an environment that fosters sharing between EPSS team members.

Informal sharing of information is critical to EPSS design and development. Often multiple team members need the same information. For example, an instructional designer who is creating a module of instruction on selling strategies will gather information. The instructional designer should share that information with the multimedia expert who is creating a video on selling. This ensures that the performer receives consistent information within and between the EPSS components.

The project manager is initially responsible for fostering the environment for sharing. Some techniques that project managers use include:

- Provide a room where team members can go to relax, post information about what they are doing (system flowcharts, status), and handouts of information they have collected or created.

- Allocate a portion of the team meeting for information sharing.

- Create an on-line bulletin board or conference for team members to share information and discuss issues.

- Encourage team members to share information through electronic mail, office visits, team lunches, and so on.

Create Communication Vehicles

Team meetings, phone calls, and e-mail keep the team's vision intact.

The project manager holds the vision for the team. The project manager typically has the closest contact with the client and performers and their respective needs. The project manager is often the conduit through which development standards, team protocol, schedule, and work assignments flow.

Initially, the project manager may have the weekly team meetings to communicate these and other team mores. The team meeting can be face to face or via audio or video teleconferencing if team members are dispersed across different worksites. As the team members begin to work together, the project manager may choose to hold meetings less frequently and use electronic mail or phone calls to communicate information.

Decide Team and Individual Work Strategies

Decide logical sub-teams based on EPSS components and team roles.

The EPSS components and the expertise of team members determine how the team works together. For example, creating a module of instruction typically involves an instructional designer to create the content, flow and sequencing, a graphic designer to create graphics and user interface and a software engineer to create the programming that links the instruction together and into the EPSS. However, if the team uses a software authoring language, the instructional designer can create the instruction, link it, and possibly integrate it into the EPSS.

Table 9-2 describes EPSS components, media formats, and instructional contexts, and the sub-teams and roles that could evolve to create items. Note that the graphic designer, usability expert, and quality control expert are ancillary roles unless specified.

Table 9-2. EPSS Team Roles and Responsibilities

EPSS Component	Roles and Responsibilities
Knowledge bases	*Instructional designer*: Research information; decide formats; sequence and write information. *Software engineer*: Design and program database; integrate database into EPSS. *Graphic designer:* Consult on user interface design. *Usability expert:* Design user interface.
Help and reference	*Instructional designer*: Decide media formats (text, video, audio, and graphics); decide instructional strategy (procedures, demonstrations, definitions, and so on); decide informational paths; write and sequence information. *Software engineer*: Create dialog boxes, hotspots, response windows; create hypertext links; link help and reference to EPSS.
Instruction	*Instructional designer*: Decide media formats (text, video, audio, and graphics); decide instructional strategy (procedures, demonstrations, definitions, and so on); write instruction using authoring software *Software engineer*: Link instruction to EPSS.

EPSS Component	Roles and Responsibilities
Coaches	*Instructional designer*: Interview experts, determine appropriate strategy (where and how expert advice is given).
	Software engineer: Create expert system, integrate expert system into EPSS.
Software tools and templates	*Usability expert*: Help determine appropriate tools and templates for specific tasks.
	Instructional designer: Decide tools and templates based on tasks; design tools and templates
	Software engineer: Program tools and templates; integrate into EPSS.
Customized applications software	*Software engineer*: Customize software for specific tasks; integrate into EPSS.

Identify Strategies for Problem Resolution

Establish a process and chain of command for problem solving before problems occur.

What happens when team members run into problems during the development process? Whom do they talk to if the learning module they've created won't run within the EPSS? What happens if the software they've purchased does not work as stated?

The project manager should create an environment that allows the team to share problems as well as achievements. If the manager is not the appropriate person to submit problems to, then delegate the responsibility to a team member. Reiterate these responsibilities. Make sure that team members know that they can raise issues about all aspects of the project – from the schedule, to timeframes, to the actual system.

Table 9-3 describes types of problems that can occur during EPSS development. As shown, the team member should escalate to the person in column two. If that person cannot solve the problem, she or he will escalate further (column three) until the problem is resolved.

Table 9-3. Problem Escalation During EPSS Development

If this is the issue...	Then escalate to...	No solution? Escalate to...
Team dynamics:		
Team member not meeting obligations	Project manager	Team member's manager
Team needs motivation	Project manager	
Team needs training	Project manager	Client
Team members not working well together	Team meeting	Project Manager
Team not sharing	Team meeting	Project Manager
Technical issues:		
Software not working	Software manufacturer	Software engineer
System integration problems	Project manager	
Team needs hardware or software	Project manager	Software engineer
Work issues:		
Timeframes unreasonable	Project manager	
Work too difficult	Project managers	
Client issues		
Reviewers not committed	Project manager	Client
Client making unreasonable demands	Project manager	Client
EPSS development issues		
EPSS component is inappropriate	Instructional designer	Project manager, client
EPSS components are not integrating well	Usability expert	Software engineer
EPSS components not matching tasks	Instructional designer	Project manager, client

Decide Parallel and Sequential Tasks

The sequencing of the EPSS development tasks depends on the EPSS, team members, and team roles.

In EPSS development, team members may depend on each other to complete job tasks. The dependencies between development tasks help determine if work should be done in parallel or in sequence. For example, suppose the EPSS contains hypertext help. Certain tasks can occur in parallel, and others must occur in sequence. In parallel, the instructional designer can collect information and format it while the software engineer creates the dialog boxes for the user interface. However, the software engineer must wait until the information is written before it can be linked to the user interface and integrated into the EPSS.

The project manager must make a list of all job tasks and decide interdependencies such as these. Using project management software, the project manager can decide what tasks can be performed in parallel or in sequence. This information is the basis of a master schedule that tracks all EPSS components from the macro- to the micro-planning levels.

Coordinate Work Hand-Offs

Project management is an intricate balancing of people, tasks, time, and budget. It is important for the project manager to decide in advance how the team will work together to accomplish tasks. For example, when the instructional designer completes a learning module, should the designer tell the software engineer where it is and let the engineer integrate it into the EPSS? Or should the instructional designer give it to the project manager first and the manager hand it to the engineer?

The project manager should ask the following questions when deciding how to coordinate work:

- Should all deliverables be reviewed by me before hand-off?

- Should quality checking by a quality assurance expert occur before each hand-off?

- Should the team members send mail or call when they hand off work, or should they report status at team meetings?

- Should I keep a master schedule of deliverables and hand-offs, or should each team member keep their own schedule?

- Can I trust my team to meet their deadlines?

Once the project manager answers these questions, the manager should communicate these expectations to all team members. Setting these expectations prevents delays in the development process and keeps the team members feeling secure about the team's progress.

Determine Work Tasks

Determine EPSS development team tasks from start to finish.

Regardless of the team size, the project manager should break the development work down into discrete tasks. This prevents any tasks from being missed. Planning to this level also gives the team intermediate successes as the work toward the final goal and identifies any task interdependencies.

Identify development tasks for:

- Each EPSS component
- EPSS component integration
- System integration
- System testing and debugging
- Performer and client involvement and sign-off
- Software master creation
- EPSS implementation

Schedule and Assign the Work

Create and maintain a master schedule that tracks all EPSS development work.

Based on the development task lists, create a master schedule. This schedule lists all tasks by topic, gives expected completion dates, and assigns the responsible team member or team members.

Assign work based on conversations with team members (their strengths, weaknesses, and career goals) and your perceptions of team dynamics. If the budget allows, assign stronger technical members to work with weaker ones to help build skills and team spirit Re-visit these assignments as the development progresses to make sure that the right people are doing the right work.

Prepare the Team for Development

A "start-up" pack-age for the EPSS team gets the team motivated and speaking the same language.

Successful EPSS teams "speak the same language." They are privy to the same information, follow the same standards, and use tools and templates that keep their work consistent.

The project manager should create a project start-up package that contains this kind of information. The project manager can hold a kick-off meeting to go over the package and begin the process of moti-vating the team.

The EPSS project start-up package should contain:

- Project plan
- Functional and design specifications
- Content materials
- Roles and responsibilities for team members
- Project contact list (names, phone numbers, and roles of all team members, client, and performers)
- Development tools and standards
- Problem resolution strategies
- Team philosophy
- EPSS philosophies and goals
- Status reporting expectations
- Team meeting schedule
- Project schedule
- Development standards (writing, software coding, and so on)
- Training opportunities and sign-up sheet

The project manager updates this information if it changes and gets it out to the team.

Develop EPSS Components

This section describes developent strategies, process, and guidelines.

EPSS development is complex, demanding, and exciting. The tenor of the development effort depends on many variables including the EPSS structure, team roles and expertise, hardware and software, client support and performer involvement.

Understanding all of the nuances of the development environ-ments that create the myriad of EPSSs could be an entire book. This book provides the following insights into the development process:

- Development strategies
- Development guidelines

Development Strategies

Development strategies include team motivation, adherence to standards, team sharing, and performer involvement.

EPSS development has the potential to be confusing and uncoordinated. However, there are strategies that the project manager and the team can use to keep the development effort smooth and seamless. These strategies are:

- Motivate the team
- Adhere to templates and standards
- Share within team and subteams

Motivate the Team

It's 8:00 p.m. and the EPSS development team is working hard. The software engineer cannot get the hypertext reference system to work. The instructional designer rushes in with one more learning module to add to the system build. The team congregates around the software engineer's desk. Will the system build?!

The project manager appears at the software engineer's office. "Everyone to the Brainstorm Barn, we need to meet for a few minutes," she says. The team reluctantly follows. The project manager herds the team into the conference room. Boxes of pizza, bottles of soft drinks, and a radio playing soft jazz music greet the team. "Dig in everyone, the system build can wait until after you eat!" There is a collective sigh of relief from the team.

A good project manager knows how to keep the team motivated. Whether it's an impromptu pizza party or positive feedback during team meetings, the project manager must find ways to keep the team focused, positive, and feeling valued.

The following are some strategies for motivating the team:

- Break development tasks down into chunks so that the team can experience small successes as they strive toward the final goal.

- Relay information about team members' contributions back to their respective managers.

- Dedicate time at each team meeting to discuss successes. Also dedicate time for "gripes" and solutions.

- Provide proper support for development – tools, training, and resources.

- Reward the team with team lunches, parties, and other surprises.

- Keep the team involved in any decision making regarding the deliverables, schedules, and client commitments.

Adhere to Templates and Standards

Tools, templates and standards keep the EPSS consistent.

EPSS development standards are the key to organized chaos during the development phase. When the instructional designer and graphic designer write hypertext using the same authoring and writing standards, the hypertext appears to be created by one person, not many. Without standards, the EPSS can be incongruous. Incongruity can lead to performer frustration and system misuse or disuse.

Encourage the team to adhere to standards, as well as update them as the change.

Table 9-4 describes the tools, templates, and standards that the team uses during the development effort.

Table 9-4. Tools, Templates, and Standards

	For Software Engineers	For Instructional Designers
Tools	Software authoring	Hypertext authoring
	Software coding	Computer-based training (CBT) authoring
	Flowcharting	Graphics
Templates	Screen layout	Screen layout
	Hypertext	CBT screen layout
		Graphics

	For Software Engineers	For Instructional Designers
Standards	Coding	Writing
	Annotating software code	Graphics
	Flowcharting	CBT storyboarding
	Filenaming	Filenaming
		Key wording
		Indexing

Share Within Teams and Subteams

Sharing information, techniques, strategies, and tools is important. Individual team members can only benefit from making the work of other team members easier. The project manager should encourage this open environment and the camaraderie that facilitates sharing. Encourage team members to send e-mail, talk frequently, and present information relative to the team at team meetings.

Development Guidelines

This section describes development processes and guidelines for the user interface, hypertext, video, and expert systems.

Creating EPSS involves developing components like instruction, coaches, user interface, and databases individually and then integrating them into one, seamless support environment.

Knowing the processes, hints, and idiosyncrasies of each of these formats and contexts helps the development effort.

The following are development guidelines for selected EPSS components, media formats, and instructional contexts.

User Interface

The user interface is integral to the performer's perception of the EPSS. The EPSS may provide the proper support, but is it easy for the performer to figure out how to get to the support? Is the EPSS linking together different tools, applications, or legacy systems, and if so, is the user interface consistent across these different areas?

Hartson and Hix have looked at the user interface design and development from different perspectives.

Table 9-5 presents some of these guidelines for user interface development.[3]

Table 9-5. User Interface Development Guidelines

Does the User Interface...	Guidelines
Center around the performer?	Know the performer
	Understand performer tasks
	Keep performer in control of system
Work consistently?	Use similar syntax and semantics
	Be consistent across different applications
	Keep unchanging options in fixed positions
	Change as little as possible from screen to screen
Work simply?	Keep simple tasks uncomplicated
	Make difficult tasks as simple as possible
	Group information that is related
	Show only information that is necessary
	Organize screens
Get performer's attention?	*Marking*: balance underline, bold and inverse video
	Size: maximum of 4 font sizes per screen; no all-uppercase characters
	Fonts: maximum of 3 different serif fonts per screen
	Blinking: use sparingly and at 2-4 hz.
	Audio: soft tones for positive feedback; harsher tones for emergencies or attention
	Color: maximum 4 different colors per screen; use conservatively; use color coding to show relationships between screen objects
Provide appropriate feedback?	Use informative feedback
	Give status information if system is doing a lengthy computation
	Use visual cues to show performers effects of

Does the User Interface...	Guidelines
	their actions and what is available on the screen
Accommodate performer differences?	Try to meet different performer needs
	Give novices a small number of meaningful functions
	Give frequent users powerful commands, ability to customize interface, concise feedback, and so on.

Hypertext

The development of hypertext information is a combination of good screen and information design. Screen and information design are discussed in this chapter and Chapter 7; *ED⁴:The Design Phase.*

Other development strategies include:

- **Keep the intent of the hypertext in mind**
  Remain true to the intent of the hypertext. In the design phase, the EPSS team decides if the hypertext will be instructional or help (reference, job-aid, and so on). In addition, be mindful of how performers will use the hypertext within their job context. Accommodate different strategies for navigating the information based on what the team knows about the performer.

- **Organize information**
  Decide a logical flow through the information, and create topics based on that flow. Flowcharting is a useful method determining the flow and relationships between topics. Flowcharting also helps establish possible paths that performers may take through the hypertext. This also ensures that the performers don't lose sight of what they are looking for and how to extract what they need.

- **Adhere to development guidelines**
  Consistency is important for any on-line medium. Glaring inconsistencies in writing style, screen formatting, and typography detract from the performer's comprehension of the hypertext message.

Video

Digital video should be used sparingly in EPSS. Development issues are complex, video files are large, and a graphic or animation may yield the same or better effect for less time and money.

However, if video is the format that best matches the task, Gayeski recommends the following process and guidelines:[4]

- **Pre-production phase**

  Create a *treatment*. This is a one-to-two page description of what the program will look like.

  Write a *script*. Cost for scripting is 10% of budget or $3000 for a program under 30 minutes.

- **Production phase**

  Shoot location video (if required)

  Add graphics, audio, and voice over narration

- **Post-production phase**

  Edit program – add transitions, sound track, special effects. Editing costs are typically one hour per finished minute of video.

Coaches

Reynolds describes a process for creating the expert systems that support coaches. The design process is similar to any software product. Table 9-6 describes a portion of the analysis, design, and development process.[5]

Table 9-6. Development Process for Expert Systems

Process Stage	Step	Notes
Analysis	1. Select suitable problem	
	2. Select development tool	
	3. Perform knowledge engineering	Can be performed by instructional designer or software engineer.

Process Stage	Step		Notes
		a. Gather pertinent knowledge	Extract information from experts through interviews.
		• Identify outcomes	
		• Identify inputs	
		• Define process	
		b. Create fact groups	Places related facts together.
		c. Develop logical chart	Shows the relationships between facts in the process.
Design		d. Develop decision tree	Represents process in the form of questions and answers.
		e. Develop matrix	Visual representation of decision tree.
		f. Write rules	Conveys process in a programmable form.
Develop	4.	Develop prototype	
	5.	Evaluate prototype	
	6.	Develop system	

Test and Revise the EPSS

Test the EPSS as each component is completed and after the entire EPSS is complete.

Complete system testing should occur during system integration and with performers.

• **Test and debug at component level**
The team should build testing in at the subteam level. Identifying and solving coding problems at the component level will mean fewer problems when the software engineer integrates the entire system.

• **Test and debug the entire EPSS**
As the software engineers complete components, the lead engineer must integrate the component into the system and test it to make sure that it works within the EPSS. (Note that the engineers are bringing tested components to the system test.)

Testing can take place weekly or as often as the project manager feels it is necessary.

- **Test with performers**
  As throughout the process, the performer is a key contributor to the development. Schedule several performer reviews. Choose performers who have varying levels of knowledge. Have the performers work through a job task to make sure the EPSS is actually functioning as needed (see Figure 9-2 for a task observation sheet).

- **Revise**
  Revise the EPSS based on system testing and small-task performer review.

Pilot Review and Revise

Have performers review the EPSS prior to completion.

At this point in the development, the EPSS components are integrated, and most functionality is in place. The project manager should prepare for a larger segment of the performer population to review the system.

The ideal review would be to prepare software kits for the performers to install on their work systems and have the performers perform actual work tasks using the EPSS.

If this is not a possibility, create an off-site laboratory situation as described earlier in this chapter in the section called *Developing the Prototype*, and have the performers work through several representative work tasks. Observe the performers.

After the observation, compile suggestions and recommendations, and implement the highest-priority ones. Revise the EPSS based on these high-priority issues.

Perform Final Quality Control Check

Perform quality control with a quality assurance expert, copy editor, and technical expert.

The EPSS should undergo a final, comprehensive quality review before building the software installation kit. Table 9-7 is a checklist of performance, technical, content, and overall quality issues that the team should check. Typically, the team members work with a quality control expert, copy editor, and a technical expert.

Table 9-7. EPSS Performance Checklist

Category	Questions
Performance	Is response time adequate?
	Does EPSS properly support work performance?
Technical	Are all components working properly?
	Is routing between EPSS components working correctly?
	Do all components meet the requirements of the detailed design?
Content	Is content accurate and complete?
Overall Quality	Is the EPSS easy to use?
	Are screens consistent?
	Is the text grammatically correct?
	Are there typos or grammatical errors?

Build the Software Installation Kit

Create a software kit (on-line media), test, and debug.

The creation of the software installation kit is the final major step in the Develop phase. In this step, the software engineer builds, tests, and debugs the software installation kit, whether on-line or on electronic or optical media. Simultaneously, the instructional designer works with the software engineer to write the installation procedure.

The team should build and test the kit, then practice-install on the performer's system (or a development system that is identical to the performer system). This tests the kit and the installation procedures. Test systems should include all hardware and software configurations that performers use.

It is important that this system not be one that was used for testing to ensure that during installation, the correct paths and parameters are defined.

The project manager should deliver the software master kit to the client and receive a sign-off approval. This hand-off signals the end of the Develop phase.

Prepare to Implement the EPSS

The team plans for implementation in the Define phase. However, the project manager should do some final preparations for implementation in this phase. The project manager should use the checklist in Table 9-8 as a final step in preparing for implementation.

Table 9-8. Pre-Implementation Checklist

Delivery Method	
Network kit	Procedure written for creating network kits?
	Installation procedures written?
	On-line directory created for storing network kits
	On-line directory location for public access given to client and performers?
Media kit	Media labels created?
	Media copying facility chosen and copying instructions ready?
	Distribution strategy communicated?
	Check copy available and ready for testing prior to mass production?
	EPSS team member prepared to verify media kits?
	Installation procedure or guide written?
On-site installation	Customer hardware and software known?
	EPSS team member ready to custom-install software?
	Customer informed of on-site installation schedule?
	Installation procedure ready to be tested?

Delivery Method	
Delivery Support	
Hotline	Support strategy (hotline account, phone line, or electronic mail line) available for customer's installation questions?
Installation Guide	Installation guide or procedure written and edited?
	Installation procedures ready to be tested?
On-site support	EPSS team member ready to provide on-site installation support as needed?
Implementation Support	
Hotline	Support strategy (hotline account, phone line, or electronic mail line) available for customer questions during early use?
	Hotline set up to log software problems, errors, wishes?
Training	Training accompanying the software?
	Training method been decided (print guide, lecture/lab, or on-line tutorial)?
	If lecture/lab, have class logistics been worked out?
On-site support	EPSS team member ready to provide support during early months of use?

Project-manage the Develop Phase

As in the Design phase, the project manager should continue to manage communications within the project team and with the client.

Manage

- **Prototype review**
  The project manager should ensure that the prototype review occurs and that it includes:

     – Matching project plan and design specification
     – Matching client and performer expectations
     – Reviewing for adherence to standards
     – Verifying for accuracy and consistency

- **Changes in project scope**
  The prototype and pilot reviews could result in a change of scope. The project manager should discuss any changes with the client and create an addendum to the project plan to cover any additional development work.

- **Pilot testing and evaluation**
  The project manager should lead the pilot and play a key role in negotiating changes with the performer, client and EPSS development team.

Document

- **Prototype and pilot test data**
  These results help measure the effectiveness of the EPSS. The project manager makes sure that the instructional designer collects and reviews these data.

- **Client's acknowledgment of the software master**
  The project manager should receive acknowledgment from the client that the client has reviewed and approved the software master.

Overcoming Obstacles

Table 9-9 describes major obstacles during the develop phase, and suggested solutions.

Table 9-9. Common Develop Phase Obstacles and Solutions

Obstacle	Solutions
Team does not have EPSS development skills	Attend an EPSS workshop or conference.
	Consult with internal EPSS experts for proven development processes.
	Modify and use the best approaches from software design for other software systems or computer-based training (CBT).
Software and hardware difficulties	Build time in schedule for hardware and software training.
	Recruit team members who are experts in the software and hardware that the team is using.
	Make full use of hardware and software support groups and hotlines.
	Choose hardware and software that is reliable, or fully test new hardware and software before the team commits to a software and hardware strategy.
Software installation difficulties	Test-install the software kit on the performer's system or a development system that is identical to the performer's.

---

1 Spitzer, Dean R. The Design and Development of Effective Interventions. In *The Handbook of Human Performance Technology,* eds Harold D. Stolovitch and Erica J. Keeps, San Francisco: Jossey-Bass, 1992.

2 Spitzer, Dean R. The Design and Development of Effective Interventions. In *The Handbook of Human Performance Technology*. San Francisco: Jossey-Bass, 1992.

3 Hartson and Hix, "Developing User Interfaces: Ensuring Usability Through Product and Process," Virginia Tech, Blacksburg, VA, 1993.

4 Gayeski, Diane M. Video-Based Instruction. In *Handbook of Human Performance Technology: A Comprehensive Guide for Analyzing and Solving Performance Problems in Organizations,* eds Harold D. Stolovitch and Erica J. Keeps, San Francisco: Jossey-Bass, 1992.

5 Reynolds, Angus. Expert Systems: Key to Performance Support. In *ASTD Handbook of Instructional Technology,* eds Harold D. Stolovitch and Erica J. Keep,. New York: McGraw-Hill, 1993.

ED⁴:

The Deliver Phase

THIS CHAPTER describes the Deliver phase, the fourth and final phase of the ED⁴ process for designing and developing Electronic Performance Support Systems.

Deliver Phase: Overview

Install and evaluate the EPSS in the deliver phase.

The result of the Define, Design, Develop, and Deliver phases is an EPSS that meets performer needs. In the Deliver phase, the EPSS team helps the performer group install and begin using the new system. The EPSS team evaluates the EPSS' performance. Also, the project manager works with the client to plan for future EPSS releases.

Table 10-1 describes the Deliver phase steps, including participants and outcomes of each step.

Table 10-1. Deliver Phase Steps

Step	Participants	Outcomes
Decide EPSS delivery medium	Software engineer, project manager, client	Network or media kit or on-site installation
Support the EPSS delivery	Software engineer, project manager, client	Hotline support, installation procedures, or On-site support
Support the EPSS implementation	Software engineer, project manager	Hotline support Implementation training
Evaluate the EPSS	Instructional designer, project manager	EPSS evaluation report
Archive the project	Project manager, project team	Completed project file, post-project review, archived project directory

Decide EPSS Delivery Medium

The delivery method can be a network or electronic media kit or on-site installation.

In the Develop phase, the software engineer creates a generic software installation kit. In this phase, the software engineer and project manager deliver the appropriate software medium.

Network Kit

The software engineer creates an on-line, public-accessible directory from which multiple people can copy the network kit (see Figure 10-1). The directory also includes clearly written installation procedures to accompany the software. The project manager provides the location of the kit and installation procedures.

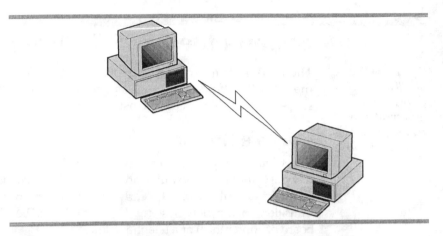

Figure 10-1. Network Kit

Media Kit

The software engineer prepares for the creation of the master kit (diskette, tape cartridge, CD-ROM, or magnetic tape – see Figure 10-2). The project manager arranges for media duplication, label creation, and duplication. The instructional designer creates installation procedures and arranges for duplication. The project manager arranges for delivery of the media kit (software media and installation procedures).

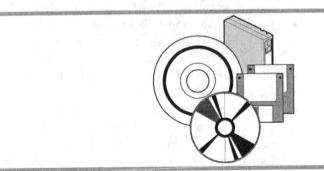

Figure 10-2. Software Media

On-Site Installation

The software specialist receives installation procedures written by the instructional designer. With prior knowledge of the performer's hardware and software environment, the software specialist installs the software kit on the performer's system.

Support the EPSS Delivery

Create a hotline, installation procedures or implementation training to support the EPSS delivery.

The project team provides support for the performers as they install the EPSS. The type of support depends on whether the team creates a software kit or does a custom installation. Here are some options.

Create a Hotline

The client and performers may need a hotline (dedicated, 24-hour response line) to answer questions as the EPSS is installed. A hotline is also very useful during the early months as the performers make the transition to the new system. The hotline can be electronic (bulletin board or conference) or a telephone line.

Create Installation Procedures

Typically, the instructional designer and the software engineer create an installation procedure to accompany the EPSS software kit. The installation procedures can be integrated into the on-line kit or can be a printed document that accompanies the kit.

Good installation procedures clearly explain each step in the process, and provide the following information for the EPSS installer:

Provide assistance during installation
- Provide help text for any questions asked during the installation
- Give an estimated time for the installation
- Include help on installation steps if needed
- Describe the privileges that the installer must have

Explain the required installation and run-time environment
- Describe how much disk space is required
- Describe what data backup or archival is required
- Describe dependencies between the EPSS and other system applications, utilities, and resources
- Explain the hardware and software environment required for the EPSS to install and run
- Explain where to install the EPSS or create the installation directories

Provide troubleshooting and run-time instructions
- Includes instructions on what to do if the installation fails
- Inform the installer when the installation is complete
- Conclude with explanation on how to run the EPSS

Provide On-Site Support

In a custom installation, a software specialist installs the EPSS.

Support the EPSS Implementation

Training, hotlines, or on-site support are critical for the first few months of EPSS use.

The client may request and the EPSS team may provide several forms of support during the early months after the EPSS installation.

Support is useful when the performers are:

- Unable to find time to learn how to use the system

- Learning to use unfamiliar or new software and hardware environment

- New to or afraid of technology
- Resistant to change

The performers may have questions, need to report software bugs or errors, or want to request enhancements or additional functionality for future releases of the EPSS.

The *Support the EPSS Delivery* section of this chapter describes hotline and on-site support. An additional support method is training.

EPSS Training

While it would seem that an EPSS would be self-supporting, performers do need help making the transition to a support environment. The help can be a brief workshop that highlights how to use the EPSS and key features, with an accompanying document (workbook or job aid) that performers refer to when they are using the EPSS independently. Another option is to build a module on how to use the EPSS into the system itself.

Evaluate the EPSS

The instructional designer evaluates the effectiveness of the system after the first few months of use.

After the EPSS team installs the system, the instructional designer prepares to evaluate the system. The instructional designer evaluates the EPSS *after* the performers have been using the EPSS for several months.

Evaluation Methods

The team can use any combination of the following methods:

- Questionnaires
- Interviews
- Observations

Evaluation Criteria and Questions

The team generates questions based on the categories included in Table 10-2. This table also includes sample questions for each category.

Table 10-2. Evaluation Questions

Category	Sample Questions
General Information	Name and address?
	What is your job title?
	List specific tasks for which you use the EPSS?
Complete	Is there appropriate EPSS support for all job tasks?
	What components do you find most (least) useful?
Consistent	Are there consistencies between user interfaces?
	Can data be shared between all EPSS components?
Accurate	Do you encounter any problems while using the EPSS?
	Is the information in the EPSS accurate?
Effective	Does *<enter name>* component meet *<enter specific name>* need?
	List needs that the EPSS does not meet.
Efficient	How is system speed and performance?
	How efficient are data storage and retrieval?
	How efficient are interactions between EPSS components?

Evaluation Findings

The team interviews or observes a representative sample of the performers, analyzes and interprets the results, and presents the findings to the client.

The findings lead to software corrections or recommendations for future releases of the EPSS. Because the team has followed the ED[4] process, corrections will be minimal, and the client can use the results of the evaluation as justification for future EPSS projects.

The completion of the evaluation signals the end of the Deliver phase.

Archive the Project

Archiving the project is critical for related project teams and for future releases of the EPSS.

When the project concludes, the team creates a master copy of all deliverables, conducts a post-project review, and closes the project file.

Create a Master Copy

The EPSS team creates a master set of all deliverables, (software, training materials, and software installation procedures), and tools, templates, and standards for the project archives.

The EPSS team also cleans up, documents (provide a list and description of all files, and a description of the project directory structure), and stores the project directories on off-line media (CD-ROM or magnetic tape). This helps the EPSS team recreate the development environment if there are future software releases or corrections.

Conduct a Post-project Review

The post-project review is a meeting of the EPSS team to discuss the project's successes, problems, and solutions. In the review, the team shares project experiences, ideas, and information that benefit current and future projects, and improve the quality, efficiency, and productivity of the development process.

The team documents the meeting in the form of a report that the team stores in the project file. The team may place the report in an on-line, shared group directory for other EPSS developers to read.

Close the Project File

The project manager makes sure the project file is complete and that it contains the following information:[1,2]

- Project plan (including any addenda)
- Financial statements, budgets, or spreadsheets
- Software design specifications
- Any memos documenting changes in project scope
- Client sign off sheets
- Results of prototype, pilot, and post-delivery evaluations
- Copy of software, training, and installation procedure masters
- Post-project review report
- Quality control checklist

Table 10-3 provides a sample project archival checklist.

Table 10-3. Project Completion Checklist

Task	Date Completed
Verify that quality control expert has reviewed and approved all project materials	
Delete all unnecessary files from the project directory	
Create a file that lists and describes all project files in the project directory	
Copy all relevant project management documents to a group directory (with explanatory listing)	
Copy all tools, templates and standards to a group directory (with explanatory listing)	
Deliver one master copy of the software installation files to the group librarian	
Backup project directory to storage media	
Remove project directory from system	

Project-manage the Deliver Phase

The Deliver phase signals the end of the ED⁴ process. The final management steps involve project closure.

Manage

- **Communications**
  The project manager makes sure all EPSS team members know the results of the project evaluation. The project manager communicates project completion to the EPSS team and the client.

- **Tracking deliverables to completion**
  The project manager is aware of the status of the software as it goes from duplication to installation and troubleshoots the process.

- **Post-project review**
  The EPSS team is responsible for capturing the successes, problems, and solutions for the EPSS development process to help inform current and future projects.

- **Maintenance of project information for updates**
  The EPSS team cooperates with the project manager to clean up and document the project directories so that another development team can recreate the development environment if there is an EPSS update, correction, or enhancement.

Document

- **Verification of master quality**
  The project manager and software engineer performs the final software check before the software is duplicated and distributed.

- **Post-project review report**
  The project manager writes the report summarizing the EPSS team process and any other pertinent information that comes out of the post- project review.

- **Completed project file**
  The project manager makes sure the project file is complete and up-to-date.

- **Archived project**
  The project manager heads the cleaning and documenting of project directories and archiving the project directory onto off-line media (CD-ROM or magnetic tape).

Overcoming Obstacles

Table 10-4 describes common obstacles in the Deliver phase and strategies for overcoming these obstacles.

Table 10-4. Common Deliver Phase Obstacles and Solutions

Obstacle	Solutions
Client does not have person to install EPSS.	Encourage client to buy on-site installation for the implementation of the EPSS.
	Make sure that installation procedures are easy to understand.
	Revise installation procedures for user installation rather than system manager installation.

Obstacle	Solutions
Performers do not have time to learn to use the EPSS.	Include on-line learning module on getting started with EPSS. Discuss issue with performers' management. Encourage management to make self-training a priority.
Performers do not have proper equipment to run EPSS.	Discuss with performers' management. Stress that negative impressions about the EPSS will result if equipment is incorrect.
Evaluation raises issues about the EPSS.	Keep a record of all performer feedback for future releases of the software.

---

1 Digital Educational Services and Publishing (ESD&P) Standard No. 18: *Archiving Project Files*, Maynard, MA., 1986.

2 Digital Educational Services and Publishing (ESD&P) Standard No. 17: *Project File Requirements*, Maynard, MA., 1986.

Maintaining EPSS

THIS CHAPTER describes how to maintain the EPSS after implementation. Maintenance includes fixing software errors and responding to performer requests. The chapter also suggests how to increase the EPSS investment and prepare for future technologies.

Managing Change: An Overview

When EPSS development ends, maintenance invariably begins. Structured maintenance is key to managing change.

Once the development team installs the EPSS and makes sure it is functioning properly, the software design and development work is over...or is it?

Performance support systems like any software product exist within a dynamic environment. While the EPSS meets current needs, those needs will change. Job definitions and work within today's volatile business environments change constantly. Working relationships between groups of performers change. Policies and procedures that affect work change. The technology that supports EPSS changes.

The software maintenance profession provides a great deal of insight into managing change. Perry defines software maintenance as follows: "Software maintenance...is the set of activities that result in changes to the originally accepted (baseline) product set. These changes consist of modifications created by correcting, inserting, deleting, extending, and enhancing the baseline system. Generally, these changes are made in order to keep the system functioning in an evolving, expanding user and operational environment."[1]

Change is inevitable. However, change does not have to be a constantly moving target that companies with EPSS "miss" more than they "hit."

Drawing on the best practices of the software maintenance profession as applied to EPSS, this chapter describes the following techniques for managing change:

- Planning for change
- Deciding change options
- Using a systematic approach

Planning for Change

Prepare for maintenance by anticipating requests, identifying risks, and dedicating resources for maintenance.

Once the EPSS is in place, performers and the customer *will* request changes. Even in the best designed system, performers will want additional functionality. They will also find software defects. Systematic approaches like ED[4]: EPSS Define, Design, Develop, and Deliver, minimize the number of requests for enhancements and fixes.

If requests do occur, here are several ways to plan for change.

Anticipate Requests

The ED[4] process focuses on the needs of performers. During the EPSS design and development process, the EPSS team records performer requests. The team prioritizes these requests and implements the highest-priority ones. The team places a copy of requests they cannot implement in the project file.

Prior to maintenance, the EPSS team organizes and analyzes these early requests. The team can predict whether performers will request these again. If so, the team can plan for programming these requests in the maintenance phase.

Identify Software Risks

The EPSS development team identifies potential problem areas. This is software coding or connections between EPSS modules that are at risk of having defects or might "break" if modified.

The team identifies software risks early in the design phase. The project manager devotes extra time and resources to minimizing risk. For example, an EPSS team may know that the complex programming and large storage requirements of a multimedia computer-based training (CBT) within an EPSS are a potential risk area. The EPSS project leader can allot extra development and testing time to the multimedia experts on the team.

However, if problem areas still exist in the implemented EPSS, software maintainers recommend performing risk management. Risk management has four components: risk identification, risk analysis, risk avoidance and contingency planning.[2]

If defects do occur, the team can use the analysis to decide how to correct the defects. If performers request changes to risk areas, the team can decide whether changes to a risk area are wise. Open conversation about risk areas and risk management within the extended team is critical. Hinley and Bennett remark, "Managers...benefited from discussions with team members and gained a greater insight into many of the technical problems and wider issues...they developed project plans which they attempted to minimize risk rather than rely on more disruptive remedial action."[3]

Allocate Funding and Resources

During the design and development process, the project manager allocates funds and resources for maintenance. Planning for maintenance early in the process guarantees that the team gives enough attention to this task.

Funding covers:

- Implementing software enhancement requests
- Correcting software problems
- Addressing potential risk areas

The software maintainers may not be the same developers who created the EPSS. The project manager organizes a team of software maintainers who are experts in EPSS software and hardware.

Deciding Change Options

Change options include maintenance, redesign, and reuse.

Like any software, the EPSS has a life span. It is created, maintained, and eventually replaced. The average life span of software is approximately seven to ten years. Even the best-designed and maintained software tends to deteriorate due to fixes, corrections, and enhancements.[4] However, software can last beyond 10 years if the developers use a structured approach, excellent software development methods, and standards.

Software maintainers must determine the status of the EPSS. At what lifecycle stage is the EPSS? Have there been many bug fixes? Were sound programming methods used? Based on the answers to these and other questions, the maintainers must decide whether to:

- Maintain
- Redesign
- Reuse

When to Maintain

Software maintenance categories are corrective, perfective and adaptive.

Once the customer site installs a software system like EPSS, the EPSS typically enters a warranty period. During the warranty period, the EPSS development team is responsible for performing the types of software maintenance described in Table 11-1.

Table 11-1. Software Maintenance Types

Maintenance Types	Description
Corrective	Changes required because of software errors
Perfective	Changes, insertions, deletions, modifications, extensions, and enhancements to system to meet evolving or expanding performer needs
Adaptive	Changes required because of changes in the environment in which the EPSS operates

According to Perry corrective and adaptive maintenance occur on an as-needed basis, and perfective maintenance occurs in one- to six-month cycles. The software maintainers release update kits to the customer. The customer may assume responsibility for software maintenance after the warranty period ends. If the customer or EPSS development team foresees environmental changes that affect the

EPSS beyond the warranty period, the customer might purchase an extended warranty.[5]

When to Redesign

Maintenance may occur over an extended period of time. Patching and adding to software causes deterioration. After seven to ten years of maintenance, the customer may opt to redesign the EPSS.

Perry recommends that managers use the following checklist to decide when to discontinue maintenance and consider re-design.[6]

1. Frequent system failures

2. Software code between seven and ten years old

3. Overly complex program structure and logic

4. Software code written for outdated hardware

5. Running in emulation mode

6. Very large modules or subroutines

7. Excessive resource requirements

8. Hard-coded parameters that are hard to change

9. Difficulty in keeping maintainers

10. Seriously deficient documentation

11. Missing or incomplete design specifications

When to Reuse

Software reusability involves using generic software coding, design, and tools to create new software. While EPSSs are created specifically for a performer group, reuse concepts are applicable during maintenance. Software maintainers can apply the techniques of the EPSS development team to aid them in enhancing and correcting the EPSS. EPSS developers document and store the following information and products in a repository. The software maintainers can re-use the following:

- EPSS design and development process innovations
- Design specifications
- Software module structure
- Software code
- Design and development tools and templates

Using a Systematic Approach

Using a systematic process for maintenance is as critical as using such a process for design and development.

Besides using excellent software coding practices and techniques, the use of a process is critical to maintaining software. Complicated software such as an EPSS can become unreliable, difficult to maintain, and easily breakable if software maintainers implement change haphazardly. For example, two performers could request conflicting changes. Implementing these changes could cause software problems. The process in Table 11-2 combines the software maintenance processes of Arthur and Perry.[7,8] The software maintenance process is similar to that of the original design and development process. The process adds a means for gathering, organizing, and prioritizing change requests.

Table 11-2. Software Maintenance Process

Steps	Description
Determine need for change	Need for change can come from performers (anticipated or requested) or from the EPSS development team.
Submit change request	Submit request in on-line or written form. Sample provided in Figure 11-1.
Analyze impact of change	Determine what impact the change will have on the existing EPSS – on hardware and software, performer work environment, documentation, related systems, and so on. Decide if change should be made.
Schedule software development	Schedule resources and time to implement the change.
Analyze and review design	Review design for software fix or new coding in context of the original design.
Code, debug, and test the changes.	Create and test the new software coding or software fixes alone and in the context of the EPSS.

Update documentation	Update design specification, programming journal, and any other docu-mentation to reflect the change in functionality.
Do performer acceptance	Test change with performers to ensure that it matches the change request.
Release change	Release the change to the customer through a software release or system patch.

Control Change

Having a change request reporting system helps you categorize and respond to requests.

Having a system for capturing and responding to change requests is important for maintaining the integrity of the EPSS. The first step is to create an on-line or written form for submitting changes. Information to capture include a tracking number, category of change (corrective, preventative, or adaptive with a severity rating), and name and phone number of the requester. Figure 11-1 is an example of a change request form.

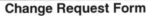

Change Request Form	
Identification Number:	4593
Requester:	Jan Dohern, Citywide Insurance
Date Requested:	5/16/94
Date Required:	5/31/94
Type:	Corrective
Severity Code:	1
System:	CityPol EPSS
Change Description:	Insurance form A102 not accepting performer input on input field 5B.
Anticipated	
Benefits:	Ability to complete form input.
Risks:	None.
Problem Location:	
Program:	ins_form
Module:	insform_a102
Resolution	Correct input field 5B.
Maintainer	George Lamonte
Start date:	5/17/94
Completion date:	5/19/94
Approved by:	Jane Larabee, EPSS Project Manager

Figure 11-1. Change Request Form

Besides a change request system, Perry gives suggestions for controlling software changes as described in Table 11-3.[9]

Table 11-3. Suggestions for Controlling Change

Suggestions
1.   Require formal (written) requests for all changes.
2.   Review all change requests and limit changes to those approved.
3.   Analyze and evaluate the type and frequency of change requests.
4.   Consider the degree to which a change is needed and its use anticipated.
5.   Analyze changes to ensure that they are compatible with the original system design and intent.
6.   Emphasize the need to determine whether a proposed change will enhance or degrade the system.
7.   Approve changes only if the benefits outweigh the risks.
8.   Schedule all maintenance.
9.   Enforce documentation and coding standards.
10.   Require that all changes be implemented using modern programming techniques.
11.   Plan for preventive maintenance.

Document the Change

Software maintainers need up-to-date, accurate documentation to do their jobs properly.

Software maintainers rely on good documentation. Documentation should exist for the life cycle of the software. Maintainers should be able to review existing design documents and any other relevant documentation.

    Documentation should be:

- Complete
- Up to date
- Accurate
- Concise
- Preferably on-line
- Always available to the maintainer

The EPSS project manager budgets for documentation and enforces its creation. Maintainers must document their work by creating change requests and maintenance reports. Maintainers must also incorporate change information into design documents. This keeps these documents up-to-date for future maintenance, redesign, or reuse.

Growing With EPSS: An Overview

EPSS allows for incremental group for customers who started small.

"Start small and grow" is a good rule of thumb for EPSS. This section describes strategies for increasing a company's investment in EPSS. There are growth strategies for those whose initial EPSS investment:

- Creating one or several EPSS components
- Creating for one or only a few performer work tasks
- Creating for one performer group
- Adding performance support within a mainframe application
- Adding EPSS to a legacy system

Adding Additional EPSS Components

After an EPSS development team successfully creates one EPSS component for a customer, the customer may be ready to consider adding additional components.

New components link to those that already exist. For example, a customer who has a hypertext information database can add (CBT). The CBT can draw from the information in the database.

Analysis is critical. The EPSS team's usability expert analyzes the effectiveness of the current EPSS component. The analysis can highlight the EPSS's positive influences on performance. When the analysis is summarized in a report, the customer can use this information to justify further investments in EPSS.

Adding EPSS Support for Additional Work Tasks

Customers whose EPSS supports only one or several job tasks may be ready to use EPSS to support additional job tasks. For example, a customer whose EPSS supports bank managers in creating performance appraisals may want to add support for the related task of determining promotion and incentive programs.

The EPSS team can assist the customer in selling the idea of further EPSS investment. The team's instructional designer can use different strategies including:

- Performing an impact analysis that projects the impact of further support based on the impact of the current system.

- Creating a prototype of EPSS support for another work task to present to senior management.

Supporting Other Performers

A customer who has a successful EPSS for one performer group may want to create an EPSS for additional performer groups. A starting point is a group that is related to the EPSS-supported group. For example, if the EPSS supports the accounts receivable group, the new EPSS components support the accounts billable group.

Strategies the EPSS team can use to help sell the concept of supporting other performer groups include:

- Directed discussion groups with the supported performer group and the potential performer group
- Prototyping
- Impact analysis
- Scoping and sizing based on the current EPSS

Converting to a Client/Server PC Environment

Encourage customers to consider the PC client/server technologies.

EPSS can exist on mainframe computers, but the client/server PC environments give an EPSS:

- Tighter integration with work tasks
- Ease of use due to more graphic user interfaces
- Better access to multimedia and hypertext technology

If a customer has an initial investment in EPSS and wishes to explore client/server PC technology, the key again is to start small. For example, the customer can start by adding several PCs to the mainframe.

Some strategies for getting customers excited about the possibilities include:

- Provide the client with demos of the possibilities.

- Accompany the client to a client/server trade show, workshop, or seminar

- Create a prototype on a PC that uses system resources on the customer's mainframe

- Have a computer analyst provide a financial and technological analysis and forecast for the customer site

- Reassure the customer that EPSS builds on existing investments in software and hardware

Moving Beyond the Legacy System

Legacy systems are usually mainframe systems and applications that need a 1990s look. These systems have user interfaces that are difficult to use and are not intuitive. Often the applications on these systems do not operate efficiently.

The customer adds EPSS to these systems to make them easier to use in support of job tasks. Often this approach is a stopgap measure so that the company does not lose its investment in existing hardware and software.

Table 11-4 provides strategies for helping the customer increase its investment in EPSS by adding to the legacy system or moving beyond the legacy system.

Table 11-4. Strategies for Legacy Systems

Adding to a Legacy System	Moving Beyond a Legacy System
Add additional components to the EPSS	Network several PCs to the legacy system

Adding to a Legacy System	Moving Beyond a Legacy System
Revise and update the user interface	Create a short range plan for system redesign using client/server technology
Create a long-range plan for system redesign using client/server technology	Get financial and technological analyses of the existing system vs. a new system

Looking Beyond EPSS

EPSS is part of an evolution in computing that includes wireless, personal digital assistants, and virtual reality.

EPSS is the cutting edge of performance intervention, *for the moment.* New technologies are on the horizon that will further advance EPSS as a concept.

Part of software maintenance is to prepare for the future – foreseeing the effect of new technologies and philosophies and preparing the resources, funding, and political support to keep software systems on the cutting edge.

The following technologies are only a sampling of what is to come. The future for EPSS will be profoundly affected by:

- Wireless technology
- Personal Digital Assistants (PDAs)
- Virtual reality

Wireless Technology

Wireless technology removes the cables that connect devices – laptops, handheld computers, and printers – to a mainframe computer. This technology creates mobile offices. Employees have access to their computer systems and colleagues from any location.

Callahan and Hyland of the Gartner Group emphasize that, "Wireless enables direct, location-independent communication – company-to-customer, worker-to-data, and worker-to-worker."[10] Wireless technology will be critical for sales persons, technicians, or any employee whose job requires them to work off-site or from customer site-to-customer site.

EPSS can play a critical role in providing much-needed support to these "mobile workers."

Wireless Technology and EPSS

The following are a few examples of how an EPSS can integrate with wireless technology.

- Sales person at a customer site can connect to the network, enter customer information into EPSS customized application software, disconnect, reconnect, receive and print the quotation.

- Computer repair person can troubleshoot a stalled printer using a laptop or handheld computer and an EPSS expert system module.

- Executives who travel extensively can use customized, EPSS-supported application software from any location around the world.

Personal Digital Assistants

Personal Digital Assistants are handheld or "palmtop" computers that allow easy, on-the-spot access to information, application software, and personal information management tools. PDAs typically use a pen stylus for writing and include handwriting recognition software to convert information that the user inputs into computer data. The concept relies heavily on wireless technology and supports the mobile worker.

PDAs and EPSS

The possibilities of integrating EPSS into PDAs are limitless. Perfomers need the same support on the "palmtop" that they need on the desktop. The challenge is to create EPSS that supports mobile computing while exploiting the vast stores of information that exist on mainframe computers.

Virtual Reality

Virtual reality immerses people in 3-D worlds that give them experiences that they might never have in real life. Virtual reality games let claustrophobics discover the joys of spelunking and children experience the sensation of bungee jumping.

Currently, game playing is a primary vehicle for virtual reality. However, companies see its potential for training and work simulations.

Virtual Reality and EPSS

The possibilities for incorporating EPSS/virtual reality training simulations are real. Edwards gives one of many possible scenarios, "For companies that deal with hazardous substances and technologies, it [virtual reality] could be used to train workers in a danger-free setting."[11]

1 Perry, William E. Quality Assurance for Information Systems: Methods, Tools and Techniques. Wellesley: QED Information Sciences, Inc., 1991.

2 Hinley, David S. and Bennett, Keith, H. "Reducing the Risks in Software Improvement Through Process-Oriented Management," IEEE, Conference Paper, 1993.

3 Hinley, David S. and Bennett, Keith, H. "Reducing the Risks in Software Improvement Through Process-Oriented Management," IEEE, Conference Paper, 1993.

4 Perry, William E. Quality Assurance for Information Systems: Methods, Tools and Techniques. Wellesley: QED Information Sciences, Inc., 1991.

5 Perry, William E. Quality Assurance for Information Systems: Methods, Tools and Techniques. Wellesley: QED Information Sciences, Inc., 1991.

6 Perry, William E. *Quality Assurance for Information Systems: Methods, Tools and Techniques*. Wellesley: QED Information Sciences, Inc., 1991.

7 Arthur, Lowell Jay, *Software Evolution: The Software Maintenance Challenge*, New York, Wiley, 1998.

8 Perry, 1991

9 Perry, 1991

10 Callahan, P. and Hyland J. "Getting Wireless Unstuck." The Gartner Group Inc., Stamford, Conn., 1993.

11 Edward, John. "Waves of the Future." *CIO*, January 1, 1994.

INDEX